THE MYSTERY OF THE KINGDOM OF GOD

The Secret of Jesus' Messiahship and Passion

ALBERT SCHWEITZER

Translated with an Introduction by

WALTER LOWRIE

Prometheus Books
Buffalo, New York

Originally published in 1914 and translated from
*Das Abendmahl—Das Messianitats und Leidengeheimnis,
Ein Skizze des Lebens Jesu*

Published 1985 by
Prometheus Books
700 East Amherst Street
Buffalo, New York 14215

Published in cooperation with
The Albert Schweitzer Fellowship
866 United Nations Plaza
New York, New York 10017

Library of Congress Card Catalog No. 85-60625
ISBN 0-87975-294-7

Printed in the United States of America

THE MYSTERY OF THE KINGDOM OF GOD

DEDICATED WITH SINCERE
RESPECT AND DEVOTION TO

Dr. H. J. Holtzmann

BY HIS GRATEFUL PUPIL
ALBERT SCHWEITZER

Table of Contents

Foreword

The welcomed reprint of this seminal work is important for several reasons.

First, it coincides with a recent revival of interest in Albert Schweitzer's thought. One only has to scan the New Testament literature produced during the past fifteen years to realize that the source springs uncovered by his studies of Jesus have now resurfaced with surprising vitality. From Jürgen Moltmann's claim that Schweitzer's rediscovery of eschatology for our age is "undoubtedly one of the most important events in recent Protestant Theology" (*Theology of Hope*, 1967, p. 37) to Lou Silberman's more recent agreement with Schweitzer that the abiding in Jesus cannot be disengaged from the apocalyptic, historical forms in which it worked itself out, it is obvious that an important new appreciation of Schweitzer's contributions to New Testament scholarship is taking place.

Second, it puts in the hands of young scholars and interested readers, often too dependent on secondary sources, a translation of one of Schweitzer's early original books. The revival is bringing with it a recognition of prior misreadings that even today remain obstacles to an accurate appraisal of his ideas. The reappearance of this neglected work may help to rectify such errors.

Third, while *The Quest of the Historical Jesus* is most often regarded as Schweitzer's definitive statement on Jesus, those who wish to know the more detailed argument for his position must turn to *The Mystery of the Kingdom of God*—something not all critics have done. It offers the first and most careful exegesis of the Gospel passages that serve as the basis for his controversial views. James Brabazon, in his outstanding book (*Albert Schweitzer: A Biography*, 1975, pp. 122-23), writes:

> If you ask English-speaking scholars the name of the book about Christ for which Schweitzer is famous, chances are they will say *The Quest of the Historical Jesus*. They may well add that it was a highly important work for its time, impressively researched, unconvincing, overemphatic, and unfortunately they have never read it.
>
> Still less have they read *The Mystery of the Kingdom of God*. The reason is partly that though it is the earlier book it was translated later, and the furor that was caused in England by the *Quest* had blown over by the time *The Mystery* arrived on the scene. It therefore seemed somewhat *déjà vu*, since the arguments it puts forward are summarized in the *Quest*.
>
> But the arguments are far more closely knit and compelling in the earlier book. The *Quest* had quite another purpose—it was designed as a survey of all the previous attempts to make historical sense of the Gospels, and Schweitzer, having already put forward his own solution in *The Mystery* . . . saw no reason to repeat his ideas in full. . . .
>
> *The Mystery of the Kingdom of God* then is the important book. Schweitzer never found cause to alter the views there expounded and though you will find scholars who claim that he was only able to hold to his theories by totally ignoring subsequent developments in theology, his introduction to the third edition of the *Quest*, written when he was seventy-five, shows that in fact he had remained closely in touch with these developments but found nothing in them to make him change his mind.

Fourth, not only does it give us valuable insight into his early development as a graduate student and his individual handling of scholarly problems, but this early example can serve as a grass roots guide to the present reconsideration of the critical-historical approach to the New Testament, a method successfully applied by Schweitzer more than eighty years ago.

Fifth, the final assessment of Schwitzer's revolutionary ideas and their full impact on biblical theology has not yet been made. The Schweitzerian interpretation is still a live option. *The Mystery* is still as much a challenge today as when it first appeared in 1901. Its pertinent claims still beckon for critical consideration and debate.

Last, the reappearance of this book is important because it underscores the simple truth of the cliché that newer is not always better nor is older passé.

Certain noteworthy characteristics of Schweitzer's methodology are reflected in this book: Schweitzer was convinced of the importance of the critical-historical approach to the Bible, a method he firmly adopted as a student at Strasbourg. He applied it in all his investigations, whether they concern Immanuel Kant, Johann Sebastian Bach, Jesus, or Paul. A rigorous review of the background research on the topic is followed by a thorough testing of his own hypothesis in the face of the facts. The efficacy of this objective approach, particularly for understanding the foundation events of the Gospels, was affirmed by Schweitzer: "What the life-of-Jesus research has accomplished cannot be praised too highly. It meant a uniquely important achievement on behalf of truth" (*Geschichte der Lebens-Jesu-Forschung*, 1913, p. 632).

Also, Schweitzer was aware of the crucial distinction

between the historical-descriptive and the theological-interpretative methods when determining facticity. They must be kept as far apart as possible. Tradition-bound biases surreptitiously overwhelm the best resolutions of sober reflection. History must be allowed its due before any mytho-poetic expression is made of the more enduring elements necessary for faith. The theological response moves on a different level of insight and discovery, but it must receive its direction from the historical. For facts *do* make a difference—often an essential one—especially to Christianity, which regards itself as a historically grounded religion.

It is apparent that although he knew the Gospels were primarily products of the faith-responses of the evangelists and early church, Schweitzer was assured in his own mind of the authenticity of the oldest traditions. This book is a challenge to those who hold that nothing clear can ever be known about Jesus and that sterile historical studies must be replaced by a literary-imaginative reconstruction. The historical may be inexorably entangled with the dogmatic but he believed sufficient reliable passages exist to support trustworthy conclusions concerning Jesus' life and mission.

If the earliest witness of the Apostles—the "canon before the canon"—must remain the true Christian norm, then biblical authority cannot rest on any so-called kerygma, for the theological-interpretive methods ultimately depend on critical-historical procedure, as Schweitzer concluded. The first step, then, in using the New Testament in any way as a theological authority must be historical rather than hermaneutical. If one does not presuppose this then the validation of scriptural witness either rests on *extra*-biblical authority or is arbitrary.

Another characteristic is Schweitzer's exclusive focus on the eschatological thrust of the lapidary sayings and acts of Jesus, the very ones that were avoided, softened, or attributed solely to the early church by former interpreters. Too strident for modern sensibilities they were pushed aside. But it is these very passages that, according to Schweitzer, hold the key to unraveling the enigmas which surround Jesus in the Gospels. If interpreters had been more willing to let these accounts speak in their own apocalyptic tongue for their own time, they would have come to a clearer understanding of the real Jesus instead of the fictionalized one who has dominated Christian theology for so long. The early church did not entirely create Jesus in its own image; it believed he was the suffering Anointed One who would usher in the soon-to-appear Kingdom because Jesus himself believed this. This is Schweitzer's momentous discovery.

Last, it is to be remembered that Schweitzer firmly believed his eschatological solution was not due to his personal interpretation but to his painstakingly working through the history of the life of Jesus; that is, the facts speak for themselves. And, more importantly, he believed that the critical-historical approach provides invaluable knowledge of Christian origins; the repository of facts it unearths about Jesus serves as a basic parameter and guide to the continued clarification of our spiritual response to, and our historical understanding of, Jesus for all times.

JACKSON LEE ICE

The Florida State University
Tallahassee, 1985

Preface

The attempt to write a life of Jesus, commencing not at the beginning but in the middle, with the thought of the Passion, must of necessity sometime be made. Strange that it has not been made earlier, for it is in the air!

The fact is that all presentations of the life of Jesus are satisfactory up to a certain point,—the inception of the thought of the Passion. There, however, the connection fails. Not one of them succeeds in rendering intelligible why Jesus now suddenly counts his death necessary, and in what sense he conceives it as a saving act. In order to establish this connection one must try the experiment of making the thought of the Passion the point of departure, for the sake of rendering the former and latter periods of the life of Jesus comprehensible. If we do not understand the idea of the Passion, may not that be due to the fact that we have formed an erroneous notion of the first period of the life of Jesus and so have precluded for ourselves in advance all possibility of attaining insight into the genesis of the Passion idea?

The last years of research have revealed on what slight grounds our historical conception of the life of Jesus really rests. It cannot be concealed that we are confronted by a difficult antinomy. Either Jesus really took himself to be the Messiah, or (as a new tendency of the study now seems to suggest) this dignity was first ascribed to him by the early Church. In either case the "Life of Jesus" remains equally enigmatical.

If Jesus really regarded himself as Messiah, how comes it that he acted as if he were not Messiah? How is it to be explained that his office and dignity seem to have nothing to do with his public activity? How are we to account for the fact that only after his public activity was ended (not to reckon the last few days at Jerusalem) did he disclose to his Disciples who he was, and at the same time enjoined upon them strict silence with regard to this *secret*? It explains nothing to suggest that such conduct was prescribed by motives of prudence or by pedagogical considerations. In the Synoptical accounts where is there even the slightest hint that Jesus wished to educate the Disciples and the people up to a knowledge of his messiahship?

The more one thinks about it the more clearly one recognises how little the assumption that Jesus took himself to be the Messiah suffices to explain his "life," inasmuch as no connection whatever results between his self-consciousness and his public activity. It may sound banal to ask the question, but it is one which cannot on that account be avoided, why Jesus never tried through instruction to raise the people up to the new ethical conception of messiahship. The attempt would not have been so hopeless as one commonly assumes, for at that time there was a deep spiritual movement going on in Israel. Why did Jesus maintain persistent silence about his conception of messiahship?

On the other hand, if one assumes that he did not take himself to be the Messiah, it must be explained how he came to be made Messiah after his death. Certainly it was not on the ground of his public activity, for this had nothing to do with his messiahship. But then again, what was the significance of the revelation of the secret of his messiahship to the Twelve and the confession before the high-priest? It is a mere act of violence to declare these scenes unhistorical. If one resolves upon such aggression, what is there then left of the whole Gospel tradition?

And withal one should not forget, that if Jesus did not take himself to be the Messiah, this means the death blow to the Christian faith. The judgment of the early Church is not binding upon us. The Christian religion is founded upon the messianic consciousness of Jesus, whereby he himself in a signal manner sharply distinguished his own person from the rank of the other preachers of religious morality. If now he did not take himself to be the Messiah, then the whole of Christianity rests—to use honestly a much perverted and abused word—upon a "value judgment" formed by the adherents of Jesus of Nazareth after his death!

Let us not forget that we are dealing here with an antinomy from which only one conclusion can be drawn, namely, that what has hitherto been accounted the "historical" conception of the messianic consciousness of Jesus is false, because it does not explain the history. Only that conception is historical which makes it intelligible how Jesus could take himself to be the Messiah without finding himself obliged to make this consciousness of his tell as a factor in his public ministry for the Kingdom of God,—rather, how he was actually compelled to make the messianic dignity of his person a secret! Why was his messiahship a secret of Jesus? To explain this means to understand his life.

This new conception of the life of Jesus has grown out of a perception of the nature of this antinomy. How far it is capable of solving the problem may be determined by the result of further discussion. I publish this new view as a *sketch,* since it belongs of necessity within the frame of this work on the Lord's Supper. I hope, however, from the criticism of its general lines to reach greater clearness with regard to many exegetical details before I can think of giving these thoughts definitive shape in an elaborated "life of Jesus."

I have generally been able only to suggest the literary foundation, as comports with the sketchy character of this presentation. Any one, however, who is thoroughly familiar with this subject will readily perceive that behind many an assertion here made there lurks more detailed study of Synoptic texts than appears at the first glance.

For the Synoptic question especially, the new conception of the life of Jesus is of great importance. From this point of view the composition of the Synoptists appears much simpler and clearer. The artificial redaction with which scholars have felt themselves compelled to operate is very much reduced. The Sermon on the Mount, the commission to the Twelve, and the eulogy of the Baptist are not "composite speeches," but were for the most part delivered as they have been handed down to us. Also the form of the prophecy of the Passion and the Resurrection is not to be ascribed to the early Church, but Jesus did actually speak to his Disciples in these words about his future. This very simplification of the literary problem and the fact that the credibility of the Gospel tradition is thereby enhanced is of great weight for the new interpretation of the life of Jesus.

This simplification rests, however, not upon a naïve attitude towards the Gospel accounts, but is brought about by insight into the laws whereby the early Christian conception and estimate of the person of Jesus conditioned the representation of his life and work. Here is a question which hitherto has not been treated perhaps systematically enough.

On the one hand it is indeed certain that the early

Church had a significant influence upon the representation of the public activity of Jesus. But on the other hand we have again in the very nature of the early Christian faith justification for the presumption that the Church did not alter the main lines of the account, and above all that it did not "fabricate facts" in the life of Jesus. For in fact the early Church maintained an attitude of indifference towards the life of Jesus as such! The early Christian faith had not the least interest in this earthly life, because the messiahship of Jesus was grounded upon his resurrection, not upon his earthly ministry, and the disciples looking forward expectantly to the coming of the Messiah in glory were interested in the earthly life of Jesus of Nazareth only in so far as it served to illustrate his sayings. There was absolutely no such thing as an early Christian conception of the life of Jesus, and the Synoptic Gospels contain nothing of the sort. They string together the narratives of the events of his public ministry without trying to make them intelligible in their sequence and connection, or to enable us to perceive the "development" of Jesus. Then in the course of time, as the eschatological expectation waned, as the emphasis upon the earthly appearing of Jesus as the Messiah began to preponderate, and thus led to a particular view (a theory) of the life of Jesus, the accounts of his public ministry had already assumed so fixed a form that they could not be affected by this process. The Fourth Gospel furnishes a historical picture of the life of Jesus, but it stands in much the same relation to the Synoptic account of the public ministry of Jesus as does Chronicles to the books of Samuel and Kings. The difference between the Fourth Gospel and the Synoptics consists precisely in the fact that the former furnishes a "life of Jesus" whereas the Synoptics give an account of his public ministry.

The faith of the early Church influenced by immanent laws the mode in which the public ministry of Jesus was represented, just as the Deuteronomic reform affected men's conception of the course of events during the period of the Judges and the Kings. It was a case of inevitable and unconscious shifting of the perspective. The new view here presented takes due account of this shifting of the perspective, and from this reckoning it results that the influence which the belief of the early Christian community exerted upon the Synoptical accounts does not go nearly so deep as we have hitherto been inclined to suppose.

Strassburg, August, 1901.

An Introduction by the Translator

I. *An Account of Schweitzer's Work and Its Reception*

The work which is here translated was published in 1901 as the *second* part of a treatise entitled *Das Abendmahl.* The full title reads: *The Lord's Super in connection with the Life of Jesus and the History of Early Christianity.* This second part was issued separately and bore also the following sub-title: *Das Messianitäts und Leidensgeheimnis. Eine Skizze des Lebens Jesu.*

It implies no disparagement of Schweitzer's novel and important study of the Lord's Supper that this second part is here separated from the first and published by itself in English. This part is really independent. It has moreover a much broader scope and appeals to a far wider interest than does the treatise as a whole. There is reason to fear that, appearing as a part of a study of the Lord's Supper and under that title, it might be ignored by many of the persons who most would desire to read it. The scant attention accorded at first to Schweitzer's work in Germany may be ascribed in part to that very cause, and there appears to be no other reason to account for the fact that the "Sketch" has not yet been publicly noticed in England or America, so far as the translator is aware.

It will not be denied, even by those who are least inclined to agree with the views of the Author, that this first work of the young Strassburg student did not deserve the oblivion which seemed to threaten it for some years after its appearance. It is manifest now that Schweitzer's theory, to say the least of it, must be *reckoned* with by every one who would seriously study the Gospels or the Life of Jesus. Obviously it was not the weakness of the book, but rather its strong originality, and in particular the trenchant way in which it demolished the "liberal life of Jesus," which accounts for the passive hostility with which it was greeted. In fact it contained more than could be readily digested at once either by a liberal or a conservative mind. Most of the New Testament students in Germany had collaborated in the fabrication of the "liberal life of Jesus" and they could not patiently endure to see their work destroyed. Those among us who fancy that German professors are bloodless beings who live in an atmosphere purified of passion and prejudice, need to be informed that on the contrary they are human, all too human. The animosities of party and school and the jealousies of the cathedra have been proverbial for generations. The reception accorded to Schweitzer's work does not seem creditable. It was met by something like a conspiracy of silence.

Schweitzer, however, *compelled* attention by the publication in 1906 of a much larger work entitled, *"Von Reimarus zu Wrede,"* which is a history of the study of the life of Jesus during the last century. A work like this, practically the only one of its sort, supplied a felt need and could not be passed by without notice. Schweitzer's own view, however, though it was presented clearly in this volume, was still not taken due account of in Germany. Jülicher's supercilious criticism in *"Neue Linien"* (190—) is characteristic of the treatment it received. The translator knows of no prominent scholar in Germany who has cordially welcomed Schweitzer's view, nor of any that has thoroughly and ably opposed it. They have been occupied there rather with Wrede's [1] acute criticism of the messianic element in the Gospels and with the denial by Drews [2] and others of the historical existence of Jesus. To destructive criticism of this sort Schweitzer's own work is the best answer. The only work which seriously reckons with this new point of view is a brief but magisterial book by H. J. Holtzmann: *Das messianische Bewusstsein Jesu,* 1907.

Very different was the reception of Schweitzer's latter work in England. The interest there centred at once upon Schweitzer's own view. In 1907, the year after its publication, Professor Sanday delivered a course of lectures at Oxford and Cambridge in which he enthusiastically accepted Schweitzer's position with hardly a reservation.[3] In 1910 this second work of Schweitzer's was translated into English and published under the title: *The Quest of the Historical Jesus,* with a preface by Professor Burkitt. By this time the interest in Schweitzer and his theory had become a furore among the younger men in Oxford and Cambridge. But just then there came an emissary from Germany, Professor Ernst von Dobschütz, who essayed to disprove Schweitzer's theory in a course of lectures delivered at Oxford in 1909.[4] Whereupon Professor Sanday, in a pathetic article in the *Hibbert Journal* for October, 1911, retracted his support of Schweitzer's position. He felt that he had been overhasty in adopting it. And so indeed it seems he was, for it appears that in preparing his lectures he had not taken the pains to read the "Sketch," that is to say, Schweitzer's first and fundamental and most carefully reasoned argument for his view.

[1] *Das Messiasgeheimnis in den Evangelien,* 1901.

[2] *Christusmythe.*

[3] *The Life of Christ in Recent Research,* 1907.

[4] *Eschatology of the Gospels,* 1910.

By the same token Canon Sanday seems to have been over-hasty in making his retraction, for he had not *yet* read the "Sketch,"—and von Dobschütz' criticism after all is not very impressive.

In America the whole question has been simply ignored. It generally takes, in fact, about a decade for an important foreign work to reach us,—except in the case of a very few scholars who have already gained our ear. According to this reckoning it is time the "Sketch" were translated. In view both of the acceptance which Schweitzer's theory has met with in England and of the opposition made to it there, it is high time that his most cogent and careful statement of his position be made known. For although Schweitzer's position is restated in his latter work already translated into English, and is there also illuminated from various sides, particularly in its relation to Wrede's work—which appeared in the same year as the "Sketch" and is so strikingly like it so far as its criticism goes and so different in its result,—yet it cannot be adequately appreciated without a study of the earlier work.

It is known that Albert Schweitzer has for some time been preparing to go as medical missionary to the Congo. But in spite of his medical studies he has recently found time to publish a brilliant "History of Pauline Study since the Reformation."[5] This is in a way a continuation of the history of the study of the life of Jesus. Here again Schweitzer has a view of his own: in all the complexity of Paul's thought he perceives a unity which is due to the pervading eschatological outlook. Fortunately, this view of his own, instead of being appended to the historical study, as in the former book, is to be published separately under the title: *Die Mystic des Apostles Paulus*. This

[5] *Geschichte der paulinischen Forschung,* 1911.

practical measure will insure that it shall not be overlooked. It is to be hoped too that it will not have to wait long for an English translation.

Professor Schweitzer found time also to prepare a new and much enlarged edition of his *Geschichte der Leben-Jesu-Forschung* (History of the Study of the Life of Jesus), which is the title by which he now more aptly describes his well known work. He has brought this history down to date, and in the short concluding chapter he suggests a number of pregnant reflections which will later be referred to in this introduction with the aim of conciliating this archæological world of Jesus' thought with our religious estimate of his person. It must be recognised from the outset that *time* is necessary for such an adjustment. The perception of the eschatological character of the Gospels is a sudden emergency: we have not yet had time to assimilate it.

At this writing Professor Schweitzer is already at work as medical missionary in Africa. It is of interest to know that his plan is to return after three years to Europe, and again after an equal period, to Africa. On account of the radical character of his critical works he was not accepted as a fellow-worker in any of the German missions and is labouring in conjunction with (though independently and at his own expense) the station of the Paris Evangelical Missionary Society at Lambarene in French Equatorial Africa—the country which used to be called the French Congo. "Schweitzer as Missionary" is the title of an article in the *Hibbert Journal* for July 1914 based upon the printed circular letters which he sends to his friends and supporters. In a letter to the translator he speaks of his efforts to mitigate the scourge of leprosy and the sleeping sickness as an example of "practical eschatology."

2. *The Significance of Schweitzer's Work*

The opportuneness of Schweitzer's eschatological interpretation of the life of Jesus appears the more manifest the more one knows of the recent history of Gospel study. To bring that out clearly is the special purpose of the Author in his *Quest of the Historical Jesus,* particularly in chapters I, XIX, and XX. It could not be done better. At all events such a task is obviously beyond the scope of this introduction. Here it need only be pointed out that Schweitzer's theory, striking as it is, did not spring into being without roots in a soil prepared for it. The eschatological question itself had been sharply brought to the fore. Contention for and against the recognition of it as an important element in the Gospels was the order of the day. All that tended to concentrate attention upon the problem of the personal consciousness of Jesus (as, in particular, Baldensperger's work),[6] was a direct preparation for Schweitzer. Johannes Weiss had already stood out as the foremost champion of eschatology in the Gospel.[7] His recognition of eschatology was confined, however, to the *teaching of Jesus*. Hence he did not avail himself of it for the solution of the historical problems. For this reason he cannot be regarded as an exponent—to use Schweitzer's phrase—of "thoroughgoing eschatology" (konsequente Eschatologie). But the solution Schweitzer proposed was already "in the air," as he said himself in his preface. That presentiment was strikingly fulfilled in the fact that in the selfsame year Wrede published a book with a title almost identical, which envisaged the same problems in the same way, only that it sought to solve them by eliminating eschatology as an intrusion in the historical narrative, thus

[6] *Das Selbstbewusstsein Jesu,* 1st ed., 1888.

[7] *Die Predigt Jesu vom Reiche Gottes,* 2d ed., 1900; also *Das älteste Evangelium,* 1903.

resulting in "thoroughgoing scepticism." Schweitzer is justified in insisting that his work and Wrede's cannot be played off against each other, but constitute a combined attack, so far as concerns the criticism of the common, liberal life of Jesus.

There is nothing audacious in Schweitzer's proclamation of the collapse of the liberal life of Jesus. He does not claim to have destroyed it, he merely attests the fact of its collapse. "The Jesus of Nazareth who appeared as the Messiah, proclaimed the morality of the kingdom of God, established the kingdom of heaven upon earth, and died in order to consecrate his work,—this Jesus never existed. It is a figure sketched by Rationalism, enlivened by Liberalism, and dressed up by Modern Theology in the clothes of historical science."[8] This fabric did not fall by reason of the strength of any attack from without, but collapsed through its inherent weakness, "shattered and cloven by the actual historical problems which one after another emerged and would not down in spite of all the cunning, art, artifice, and force" which was expended upon this picture of Jesus during the last hundred years. In spite of the protestation that this picture still stands undemolished, no one can be found any more to write a liberal life of Jesus. On the other hand sceptical works have multiplied so rapidly that it would be difficult to enumerate them here. After Kalthoff[9] and Drews[10] the designation of "thoroughgoing scepticism" can hardly be applied to Wrede's theory. All the books of this class owe what appearance of strength they have, not to their inherent worth, but to the weakness of the theory which opposes them—the current liberal life of Jesus. Solely with a view

[8] *Quest of the Historical Jesus,* chap. XX.
[9] *Das Christus-Problem,* 1902.
[10] *Op. cit.*

to maintaining the integrity of this picture it has been found necessary from time to time to sacrifice so much of the documentary evidence—the Synoptic Gospels or their sources—upon which the history of Jesus reposes, that in the end it seems not very unreasonable for Drews and others to assume, from the admissions of their opponents, that there is no convincing historical evidence for the existence of Jesus, and that the real task of the scholar is to show how such a figure was invented.

"It is extraordinary," says Schweitzer in the last chapter of the new edition of his History of the Life of Jesus Study, "how it has fared with the study of the life of Jesus. It set out to find the historical Jesus, and fancied that when he was found he could be set, just as he is, in the midst of our age as Teacher and Saviour. It loosed the bands which fettered him to the rock of ecclesiastical dogma, and rejoiced when life and movement returned to the figure and the historical man Jesus was seen approaching. He did not stay, however, but passed our age by and returned again to his own. That is what astonished and alarmed the theology of the last decades,—that by no violence of misinterpretation could they succeed in keeping him in our age, but had to let him go. He returned to his own age with the same necessity that the freed pendulum swings back to its original position.

"The historical foundation of Christianity, as rationalism, liberalism, and modern theology count it, exists no longer,—which, however, is not to say that Christianity has therefore lost its historical foundation. The work which historical theology believed it must carry out, and which it sees falling to pieces at the very moment when the completion was near, is only the terra cotta veneer of the true, indestructible, historical foundation, which is independent of any historical knowledge and proof—simply because it is there, it exists.

"Jesus is something to our world because a mighty stream of spiritual influence has gone forth from him and has penetrated our age also. This fact will be neither shaken nor confirmed by an historical knowledge.

"One fancied he could be more to our time by the fact that he entered it vitally as a man of our humanity. That, however, is not possible. For one reason, because this Jesus never so existed. Also, because historical knowledge, though it can clarify spiritual life already existing, can never awaken life. It is able to reconcile the present with the past; to a certain degree it can transport the present into the past; but to construct the present is not within its power.

"One cannot estimate highly enough what the study of the life of Jesus has accomplished. It is a great and unique demonstration of veracity and love of the truth,—one of the most significant occurrences in the whole spiritual life of mankind. What the modern-liberal and the popularising investigation has done, in spite of all its errors, for the present and for the coming state of religion can only be measured when one takes into comparison the Roman Catholic—or more broadly the Latin—culture and literature which has been touched little or not at all by the influence of these spirits.

"And yet the disillusion had to come. We modern theologians are too proud of our historical learning, too proud of our historical Jesus, too confident in our faith in what our historical theology can spiritually contribute to the world. The notion that by historical knowledge we can construct a new and vigorous Christianity and let loose spiritual forces in the world dominates us like a fixed idea and does not permit us to perceive that all we have done thereby is to assail, not the great religious problem itself, but one of the problems of general culture which is entrenched in front of it, and which we would solve as well as we can. We thought that we had to lead our age as it were through a by-path, through the historical Jesus,—in order that it might come to Jesus who is present spiritual power. The by-path is now barred by real history.

"We were in danger of putting ourselves between men and the Gospels and not leaving the individual any longer alone with the sayings of Jesus.

"We were in danger, too, of presenting to them a Jesus that was too little, because we had forced him into man's measure and into the mould of average human psychology. Read through the 'lives of Jesus' since the sixties and behold what they have made of the imperial words of our Lord, what a weak and ambiguous sense they have put upon his peremptory, other-wordly requisitions, in order that he might not clash with our ideals of civilisation and his other-worldliness might be brought to terms with our this-worldliness. Many of his greatest words one finds lying in a corner, a heap of discharged spring-bolts. We make Jesus speak with our time another language than that which passed his lips.

"Thereby we ourselves became impotent and deprived our own thoughts of their proper energy by transposing them into history and making them speak to us out of antiquity. It is nothing less than a tragedy for modern theology that it confounds with history everything it attempts to expound, and is actually proud of the virtuosity with which it contrives to discover its own thoughts in the past.

"Therefore there is hopeful significance in the fact that modern theology with its study of the life of Jesus, however long it may resist by the invention of fresh shifts and expedients, must in the end find itself deluded in its manufactured history, overcome by real history and by the facts—which according to Wrede's fine saying are often more radical than theories.

"What is the historical Jesus to us when we keep him clear of any admixture of the present with the past? We have the immediate impression that his person, in spite of all that is strange and enigmatical, has something great to say to all ages, as long as the world endures, may views and knowledge change never so much, and that it means therefore to our religion also a far-reaching enrichment. It behooves us to bring this elementary feeling to a clear expression, so that it may not soar away in dogmatic assertions and phrases and beguile historical science ever anew into the hopeless undertaking of modernising Jesus by diluting or explaining away what is historically conditioned in his preaching, as though he would become more to us thereby.

"The whole study of the life of Jesus has in fine only the one aim, of establishing the natural and unbiased conception of the earliest accounts. In order to know Jesus and to apprehend him there is need of no preparatory erudition. It is also not requisite that a man comprehend the details of Jesus' public ministry and be able to construct with them a 'life of Jesus.' His nature, and that which he is and wills, appears in certain lapidary expressions of his and forces itself upon us. One *knows* him without knowing much about him, and apprehends the eschatological note even if he attain no clear conception of the details. For this is the characteristic thing about Jesus, that he looks beyond the perfection and blessedness of the individual to the perfection and blessedness of the world and of an elect humanity. His will and his hope is fixed upon the Kingdom of God."

It is much to be wondered at that conservative scholars have not generally recognised the strong constructive consequences of Schweitzer's theory,—in particular the proof it incidentally affords of the historical worth of the Synoptic Gospels. Schweitzer rehabilitates the credit of

S. Mark's Gospel simply by showing that no important parts of it need be discarded on the ground that they are inconsistent with the sketch which he draws of the history of Jesus. When it is objected to him that he bases his view upon "the weakest passages," it is time we make clear to ourselves that "strong" and "weak" in this connection mean no more than *consistent* or *inconsistent* with the *assumptions* of the modern "liberal life of Jesus." It is only a roundabout way of begging the question. Generally speaking, such a document as Mark, antecedent to any theory we may attempt to apply, must be presumed to be of pretty equal value throughout. That theory which, without artifice or violence, best accords with the greatest number of facts recorded, and so best preserves the credit of the documents upon which it seeks to found itself, is presumably the right theory. Schweitzer's view, as he himself says in the Preface, greatly simplifies and clarifies the Synoptic problem. It is no longer necessary to attribute so much to "the editor's hand." The Sermon on the Mount, the Charge to the Twelve, and the Eulogy over the Baptist are not collections of scattered sayings, but were in the main delivered as they have come down to us. Especially important is the recognition that even for constructing the history of Jesus Mark by itself does not suffice: the discourses in Matthew are invaluable indications.

Nor is this the only positive and comforting element in Schweitzer's view. In the Postscript he has himself laid stress upon the aim of his work: "to impress upon the modern age and upon modern theology the figure of Jesus in its overwhelming heroic greatness." And this he has accomplished in unexpected ways. The figure of Jesus which we have striven so hard to bring into nearness and sympathy through our psychological analysis has eluded our grasp, and under the hands of the historian and archæologist it has receded inexorably into the remote past and into a corner of Galilee. It looks to us strange and even petty in its remote Galilean surroundings. Now that figure, by the force of an elemental energy, is seen to break the shackles which would bind it to a particular time and place and become—not modern, indeed, but—universal.

One may easily be so much absorbed with the difficulties in the way of accepting Schweitzer's construction as to ignore the light which it sheds upon some of the major difficulties of the traditional view with which we have long wrestled in vain. One may mention at least eight obscure points which are illuminated for the first time by the eschatological view of the Gospel history. 1. Jesus' use of the title "Son of Man,"—commonly in the third person and with a futuristic sense, as denoting a dignity and power which were *not yet* his. Jesus was the Messiah designate. 2. The position of John the Baptist: it was Jesus alone that discovered in him the character of Elijah "the Coming One" (cf. Jn. 1:21). 3. The conception of the Kingdom of God as a *gift,* to be received passively as by a little child—and yet as a thing that "violent men" must wrest to themselves "by force." 4. The relation of Jesus' messianic expectation to that which was current among the people. Jesus moralised the popular eschatological ideal by combining it with the preaching of the Prophets. That Jesus opposed a purely moral ideal to a popular political agitation is doubly a fiction. 5. The significance of the Mission of the Twelve and its connection with the popular excitement which drew five thousand men into the desert by the seashore. 6. The significance of the Transfiguration, coming *before* the Confession of Peter, and explaining how the knowledge of Jesus' Messiahship was given by divine revelation. 7. The character of the secret which Judas possessed and was in a position to betray. Our notion that during the last days in Jerusalem every one knew of Jesus' claim to be the Christ is plainly contrary to the record. The famous disputes of those days would have taken a very different form if the question which agitated all minds was, Is he the Christ? or is he not? 8. Jesus' notion of the *necessity* of his death, his resolution to die at Jerusalem, and his conception that he was giving his life as "a ransom *for many.*"

Unquestionably it is no easy matter to assimilate so novel and striking a view as that of Schweitzer. To bring it into relation with the presuppositions of our religious view in general involves demolition and reconstruction—a labor heavy and grievous to the soul. The mind instinctively recoils from such a labour and is fain to protect itself by a general repudiation and denial. Moreover the Author has presented his view with a naked simplicity which, while it renders it easier to understand and more difficult to confute, makes it also, one must confess, more difficult to accept. We are not inclined to accept opinions in the face of a display of force, and as it were at the muzzle of a gun—even when the gun is loaded with logic. Practically we must first contrive to see how the opinions may be made acceptable. This task the Author has not unreasonably left to us,—although a careful study of his work will reveal many suggestions helpful to this end. The translator has read this little book not once but many times and through a course of years, with ever increasing appreciation of its worth—not only in view of its logical force but of its *acceptability*. On the other hand, many of us have felt that the liberal life of Jesus was becoming increasingly more *unacceptable.*

Canon Sanday confesses[11] that he recoils from Schweitzer's view chiefly on account of his "tendency to push things to extremes at the dictates of logical consistency." It is *too* "thoroughgoing." It seems indeed as though the Author were inclined to press this word to an extreme, proposing to explain *all* the words and acts of Jesus with reference to his eschatological outlook. But that is only a threat. What he *has* done falls very far short of it, and it is upon *that* we have to pass judgment. *That,* in fact, is "thoroughgoing" enough to justify the term even if it went no further. The principle of "thorough" might very well apply to the construction of the history as a whole without implying that every trait of Jesus' life and teaching was coloured by it and that he himself was so obsessed by a single idea that he was unable to see things as they are. This is precisely what the Gospels do not permit us to believe. It is manifest that Jesus had a peculiarly acute sensibility to his surroundings, whether it were nature or human society, and responded feelingly, spontaneously. His sense of right and wrong was so clearly intuitive that he could deal sovereignly with the Law. Schweitzer himself furnishes suggestions which tend to render even the word "Interimsethik" acceptable. Jesus' moral teaching was oriented towards the coming Kingdom. It was "penance" in preparation for the Kingdom of God. But it was not for all this an arbitrary penance: like the ethics of the Prophets it was the prescription of righteousness. In one sense at least, it was not of merely transitory importance. From the expectation of the approaching Kingdom it received a sharpness of emphasis which it could not otherwise have had,—but it was a *true* emphasis. It described the conduct appropriate to

[11] *Hibbert Journal,* Oct., 1911, p. 84.

man in this present world *so long as this world shall last*—a conduct which is justified here by the expectation of a better world to come, "beyond good and evil" if you will.

"Thoroughgoing eschatology" is surely not incompatible with the recognition of a deeper intuition in Jesus which is necessary to explain the intensity of this very eschatology itself. It would be a rigorous extreme indeed which would exclude the recognition of Jesus' God-consciousness—his consciousness of God as Father—as the primary and all-controlling fact of his religious experience. Nothing is more obvious than that out of that consciousness he acted and spoke *immediately*. And when his acts were influenced and his speech coloured by the eschatological outlook, what was that ultimately but the consciousness of God's *nearness*? How could the expectation of a divine world be so constant and so vivid without the feeling that it is in a sense locally near, imminent, impending, ready to break in, indeed actually intruding upon this present world, as it were "the finger of God" touching us here? Intuitional feeling, presentiment, insight, does not readily distinguish between nearness in time and in space. Jesus' eschatology was an expression of his God-consciousness—the most eminent expression of it.

Eschatology in the strict sense, with all its apocalyptic features, has long ago passed out of our view of the world. Schweitzer shows us with what justification the Church discarded it. But the feeling that was behind it remains, and still constitutes the fundamental experience of religion. It is the feeling of a divine environment, close to us, unspeakably close, imminent, intruding even upon the everyday world.

"This is the finger of God,
The flash of the will that can,

Existent behind all laws,
That made them, and lo! they are."

Intuitional feeling is not especially inclined to express the sense of God in terms of time. Space is the category more familiar to it. Wordsworth finds terms to express what is so intangible.

"Those obstinate questionings
Of sense and outward things,
Fallings from us, vanishings;
Blank misgivings of a creature
Moving about in worlds not realised
High instincts, before which our mortal nature
Did tremble like a guilty thing surprised."

Apocalyptic eschatology no one could even wish to revive. But this does not mean that Biblical eschatology—the expectation of the great Event—must be dissolved in the modern hope of the gradual amelioration of the world in the course of historical evolution. We cannot but feel how great a breach that would constitute between our thought and the mind of Jesus. Schweitzer remarks upon the heavy dose of "resignation" which such a view implies. Strange that we do not more often realise this! Does our optimism blind us to the fact that we shall not partake in "the far off divine event"—except our spirit survive the bodily death? *There*—in the hope of life beyond death—is the expectation which we substitute for apocalyptic eschatology,—a substitution so natural that it came about without observation. St. Paul lived in the expectation of the coming of the Lord, but he evidently felt no sense of incongruity when he expressed the feeling that "to depart and be with Christ is very far better"—he was referring to the natural death of the body and the hope of life immediately beyond it. This is the hope which has ever since characterised the Christian Church. To dwell upon that hope, to set our "affections upon things above, where Christ is, seated at the right hand of God" —that is "heavenly mindedness." With respect to the feeling at the base of it, it is not so very different from apocalyptical eschatology. In this view Christian ethics still remains "conditional"—you may call it *Interimsethik* if you like. The conduct it requires of us is conditioned by the hope of a future life and is absurd under any other supposition. "The practice of the presence of God" is the most fundamentally important religious exercise. But if we succeed in persuading ourselves that here and now we have the only kingdom of God we shall ever know; if all our interest and effort is absorbed in realising a kingdom of God upon earth; then not only have we need of "resignation," but we cannot avoid feeling the breach between our thought and activity and that of Jesus. We are puzzled to distinguish between worldly and heavenly mindedness because even our religious interest is focussed upon this earth, as the sphere not only of our moral duty but of our ultimate hope—the gradual evolution of a perfect human society. That is what we have made of the Kingdom of God, interpreting it uneschatologically. Is not this after all a more credulous hope than that which expects a divine intervention, a "regeneration" of heaven and earth, which shall prepare the fit abode for the perfect society? And does it not strike at the very roots of the religious sentiment when we distract the mind from its natural interest and curiosity about the Beyond? Our personal fate is not so much involved in the far off amelioration of human society as in something much nearer, very near and imminent, the estate just beyond death. It is not altogether without reason that in Christian dogmatics the name of eschatology has been applied to this topic. The earlier type of eschatology Jesus himself has rendered forevermore impossible. It is likely that the first objection *we* feel to apocalyptic eschatology lies in the fact that it was expressed in terms of an erroneous cosmology and is therefore incompatible with our modern view of the world. But as a matter of fact apocalyptic eschatology vanished from the vital creed of the Church long before the cosmology upon which it was founded was proved to be false. It was Jesus who brought it to an end. Another sort of eschatology promptly took its place—another heavenly hope, which was substantially not apocalyptic. Yet this doctrine too—the early Christian notion of the soul and of heaven—was necessarily founded upon the opinions of ancient science. The doctrine of the soul and the doctrine of heaven, being less directly affected by the findings of modern science, have been more slow to change in conformity with our changed view of the world than has, for example, the doctrine of creation. But in their old form they are none the less incompatible with our modern thought; and for this reason we feel forced to put *every* sort of eschatology aside, we are no longer able to place the heavenly hope, and the heavenly mindedness which it prompts, in the central position which belongs to them. That is to say, we urgently need to express the Christian doctrine of the soul in terms of the highest modern psychology and to express our heavenly hope in terms of a modern cosmology. We need a new cosmology! That may seem to express an unpractical and fantastic desire. But it will not so seem to any one who knows what his theory of the soul and his grandiose cosmology meant practically and religiously to Gustav Theodor Fechner,[12] or who has experienced what this may mean for the orientation of his own personal religion. The old view of the

[12] *Vide The Living Word* by Elwood Worcester, 1908.

world has passed away: we have been too slothful and cowardly to take full possession of the new. There is really nothing in the modern view of the world which effectually precludes us from directing our hope and orienting our life towards the Beyond, as did Jesus in his way, and as the early Church did in its way. From the moment that Jesus passed into the invisible and was there felt and recognised as the correspondent of our religious faculty we find that spatial terms better express the substance of our heavenly mindedness than do temporal. We "seek the things that are above, where Christ is, seated on the right hand of God." To recognise that our "citizenship is in heaven" is not to render ourselves inept for the performance of our duty upon earth. Rather it needs to be reflected whether, without the detachment, without the superiority to earthly circumstance, happy or untoward, which comes from setting our "mind on the things that are above," we possess any fulcrum for doing a real work upon the world.

The eschatological interpretation of the Gospels does not thrust Jesus so far from us as we are prone to think: rather it calls us to approach nearer to him, to share again more closely "the mind which was in Christ Jesus" and which in one form or another has been at all times the chief inspiration of the Church.

In his "Concluding Reflections" Schweitzer says: "Every full view of life, cosmic philosophy, *Weltanschauung* (the German word it is impossible to translate) contains side by side elements which are conditioned by the age as well as others which are unconditioned, for it consists in the very fact that a penetrating *will* has pervaded and constituted the conceptual material furnished it by history. This latter is subjected to change. Hence there is no *Weltanschauung,* however great and profound it may be, which does not contain perishable material. But the will itself is timeless. It reveals the unsearchable and primary nature of a person and determines also the final and fundamental definition of his *Weltanschauung*. May the conceptual material alter never so much, with consequent diversity between the new *Weltanschauung* and the old, yet these in reality only lie just so far apart as the wills which constitute them diverge in direction. The differences which are determined by the alteration of the conceptual material are in the last analysis merely secondary in importance, however emphatically they may make themselves felt; for the same will, however different be the conceptual material in which it manifests itself, always creates *Weltanschauungen* which in their nature correspond with one another and coincide.

"Since the time when man attained the conditions precedent to such an apprehension and judgment of things as we might call in our sense a *Weltanschauung*—that is, since the individual learned to take into consideration the totality of being, the world as a whole, and to reflect as a knowing and willing subject upon the reciprocal relations of a passive and active sort which subsist between himself and the All—no far-reaching development has really occurred in the spiritual life of humanity. The problems of the Greeks turn up again in the most modern philosophy. The scepticism of to-day is essentially the same as that which came to expression in ancient thought.

"The primitive, late-Jewish metaphysic in which Jesus expressed his *Weltanschauung* aggravates exceedingly the difficulty of translating his ideas into the formulas of our time. The task is quite impossible so long as one tries to accomplish it by distinguishing in detail between the permanent and the transitory. And what results as the consequence of this procedure is so lacking in force and conclusiveness that the enrichment it contributes to our religion is rather apparent than real.

"In truth there can be no question of making distinction between transitory and permanent, but only of transposing the original constitutive thought of that *Weltanschauung* into terms familiar to us. How would the Will of Jesus—apprehended in its immediateness, in its definiteness and in its whole compass—how would it vitalise our thought material and construct from it a *Weltanschauung* of so moral and so mighty a sort that it could be counted the modern equivalent of that which he created in terms of the late-Jewish metaphysics and eschatology?

"If one tries, as has been done hitherto almost invariably, to reconcile Jesus' *Weltanschauung* with ours any way it will go—which can be accomplished only by paring away all that is characteristic—this procedure strikes also at the will which is manifested in these conceptions.

"It loses its originality and is no longer able to exert an elemental influence upon us. Hence it is that the Jesus of modern theology is so extraordinarily lifeless. Left in his eschatological world he is greater and, for all the strangeness, he affects us more elementally, more mightily than the modern Jesus.

"Jesus' deed consists in the fact that his original and profound moral nature took possession of the late-Jewish eschatology and so gives expression, in the thought material of the age, to the hope and the will which are intent upon the ethical consummation of the world. All attempts to avert one's vision from this *Weltanschauung* as a whole and to make Jesus' significance for us to consist in his revelation of the 'fatherhood of God,' the 'brotherhood of man,' and so forth, must therefore of necessity lead to a narrow and peculiarly insipid conception of his religion. In reality he is an authority for us, not in the sphere of knowledge, but only in the matter of the will. His destined rôle can only consist in this, that he as a mighty spirit quickens the motives of willing and hoping which we and our fellowmen bear within us and brings them to such a height of intensity and clarity as we could not have attained if we were left to ourselves and did not stand under the impression of his personality, and that he thus conforms our *Weltanschauung* to his own in its very nature, in spite of all the diversity of thought material, and awakens in it the energies which are active in his.

"The last and deepest knowledge of things comes from the will. Hence the movement of thought which strives to frame the final synthesis of observations and knowledge in order to construct a *Weltanschauung* is determined in its direction by the will, which constitutes the primary and the inexplicable ultimate essence of the persons and ages in question.

"If our age and our religion have not apprehended the greatness of Jesus and have been frightened back by the eschatological colour of his thought, this was due only in part to the fact that they could not accommodate themselves to the strangeness of it all. The decisive reason was another. They lacked the strong and clear stamp of a will and a hope directed towards the moral consummation of the world, which are decisive for Jesus and for his *Weltanschauung*. They were devoid of eschatology,—using the word here in its broadest and most general sense. They found in themselves no equivalents for the thoughts of Jesus, and were therefore not in a position to transpose his *Weltanschauung* from the late-Jewish terms of thought into their own.

"There was no answering chord of sympathy. Hence the historical Jesus had to remain strange to them to a very great extent, and that not only with respect to his thought material but also with respect to his very nature. His ethical enthusiasm and the immediateness and might which characterised his thought seems to them excessive because they know nothing that corresponds to it in their own thought and experience. So they were constantly intent upon making out of the 'enthusiast' a modern man and theologian duly observant of metes and bounds in all his doings. Conservative theology, like the older orthodoxy to which it is akin, was not able to do anything with the historical Jesus, because it likewise makes far too little of the great moral ideas which in his eschatology were struggling for life and practical expression.

"It was therefore the lack of an inward tuning to the same pitch of will and hope and desire which made it impossible to attain a real knowledge of the historical Jesus and a comprehensive religious relationship with him. Between him and a generation which was lacking in all immediateness and in all enthusiasm directed towards the final aims of humanity and of being, there could be no lively and far-reaching fellowship. For all its progress in historical perception it really remained more estranged from him than was the rationalism of the eighteenth and the beginning of the nineteenth century, which was brought closer to him by its enthusiastic faith in the possibility of rapid progress towards the moral perfection of humanity."

I marvel that Schweitzer in his "Concluding Reflections" can dwell so insistently upon one side of Jesus' eschatology and ignore so completely the other. Jesus' eschatology, the white light of his conception of the Kingdom of God, has come to us through the medium of history refracted in two rays of different colour and of different direction. One represents more specifically the otherworldly side of Jesus' preaching, the hope of eternal blessedness beyond death,—which the dogmatic theologians are pleased to call "eschatology," as though our modern idea really reflected Jesus' conception in its totality. Commonly this is what we understand by the "Kingdom of Heaven." To denominate the other ray, Schweitzer has appropriated (with as questionable a right) the "Kingdom of God." He means to indicate by this simply the moral development of humanity, here and under present terrestrial conditions. We readily understand what he means, because that is what *we* mean commonly by "the kingdom of God upon earth." We are convinced that the progress of mankind in true worldly culture and civilisation constitutes a high moral aim which we dare not relinquish; but we have all experienced the difficulty of reconciling this secular enthusiasm with the other-worldliness of Jesus. Schweitzer helps us in a measure to surmount this difficulty. He also makes it in a measure clear to us *how* (for the fact itself was patent) this enthusiasm for the progress of humanity has been reinforced by Jesus' preaching. But it is a mistake to expect of this one coloured ray that it can ever give back to us the whole white light of Jesus' inspiration. We cannot return again to Jesus' conception. History stands in the way—real history, not written narrative. Nor shall we ever be able to combine again in one white light the "broken lights" which have come to us from his teaching. But we have the two rays, and in their separateness they are both familiar to us. Our eyes bear better the coloured light. Celestial blue denotes the heavenly hope; red will do for this earth and our passionate hopes for its betterment. But why behave as if we had only one colour and all of Jesus' light must be forced into that? Schweitzer ignores the heavenly hope (the thought of life beyond death) as though it were no longer open to the modern man. One may get a notion of what it still may mean to the modern scientific mind from Gustav Theodor Fechner's *Büchlein vom Leben nach dem Tode,* or more largely from his *Zend-Avesta,* or his *Tagesansicht.* Though to be sure it can mean nothing to one who is bound by a materialistic philosophy. At all events it is certain that Jesus' will and aspiration can be much more readily and fully expressed in these terms than in the terms of ethical and social progress here below. To translate his thought into these terms requires no elaborate effort. The first generation of his disciples did it without knowing what they did. Schweitzer himself observes in another place that our modern faith in the final but slow perfection of the world "requires a larger dose of resignation" than most people are aware. And how can any perfection upon this earth be final, since none can be eternal?

We are all of us feeling after a solution of our modern difficulties. Schweitzer's effort after a tolerable accommodation is poignantly personal like ours—and like ours it is tentative. It is too early to hope for complete satisfaction. Yet his efforts obviously tend in the same direction as ours. Schweitzer perceives that "in the last resort our relation with Jesus is a mystical one." For the sake of this acknowledgment, as well as for other reasons which will be evident, I am fain to conclude this Introduction with Schweitzer's own words—the words with which he concludes his latest book:

"In the last resort our relationship to Jesus is of a mystical sort. No personality of the past can be installed in the present by historical reflection or by affirmations about his authoritative significance. We get into relation with him only when we are brought together in the recognition of a common will, experience a clarification, enrichment, and quickening of our will by his, and find ourselves again in him. In this sense every deeper relationship between men is of a mystical sort. Our religion, therefore, so far as it proves itself specifically Christian, is not so much 'Jesus-cult' as Jesus-mystic.

"It is only thus that Jesus creates fellowship among us. It is not as a symbol that he does it, nor anything of the sort. In so far as we with one another and with him are of one will, to place the Kingdom of God above all, and to serve in behalf of this faith and hope, so far is there fellowship between him and us and the men of all generations who lived and live in the same thought.

"From this it will be manifest also in what way the free and the confined movements of religion which now go side by side will come together in unity. False compromises are of no avail. All concessions by which the free conception seeks to approach the confined can only result in ambiguity and inconsequence. The differences lie in the thought material which is presupposed on either side. All efforts after an agreement in this sphere are hopeless. These differences appear so prominent because there is a lack of elementary and vital religiousness. Two threads of water wind along side by side through the boulders and gravel of a great stream bed. It is of no avail that one seeks here and there to clear out of the way the masses that are piled up between them, in order that they may flow on in one bed. But when the water rises and overflows the boulders they find themselves together as a matter of course. So will the confined and the free spirit of religion come together when will and hope are directed again towards the Kingdom of God, and the fellowship with the spirit of Jesus becomes in them something elemental and mighty, and they are thereby brought so near together in the essence of their *Weltanschauung* and religion that the differences of thought material still exist indeed, but sink beneath the surface, as the boulders are covered by the rising flood and in the end barely glimmer out of the depths.

"The names by which Jesus was called in the thought material of late Judaism—Messiah, Son of Man, and Son of God—have become to us historical parables. Even when he applied these titles to himself, this was an historically conditioned expression of his apprehension of himself as a commander and ruler. We find no designation that might express his nature for us.

"Unknown and nameless he comes to us, as he approached those men on the seashore that knew not who he was. He says the same word: But do thou follow me! and he sets before us the tasks which we in our generation must accomplish. He commands. And to those that obey him, wise and unwise, he will reveal himself in what may be given them to experience in his fellowship of peace and activity, conflict and suffering, and as an unutterable secret they shall come to know who he is." . . .

Rome, 1913

CHAPTER I

The Modern "Historical" Solution

1. *Summary Account of It*

The Synoptical texts do not explain how the idea of the Passion forced itself upon Jesus and what it meant to him. The speeches of Peter and Paul viewed the Passion in the aspect of a divine necessity which was prophesied by the Scripture. The Pauline theory likewise has nothing to do with history.

Therefore the idea of the Passion as it is developed here in connection with an account of Jesus' life is not directly furnished by the texts but is deduced from them by implication. One is left here to the unavoidable necessity of formulating a theory, the truth of which can only be judged by the measure of clearness and order which it introduces into the Synoptic accounts.

All of the theoretical constructions which have an outspoken historical interest coincide in an alleged solution which we denominate the modern-historical. What is historical about it is the interest which prompts the endeavour to explain history. The modern factor in it is the psychological sympathy of comprehension by the help of which one endeavours to show how, under the impression of particular experiences, the idea of the Passion forced itself upon Jesus and was given by him a religious significance. This solution is based upon the following considerations:

For Jesus there could be no question of constituting a ground for the forgiveness of sins. That he already assumed, as the petition in the Lord's Prayer shows,—it flowed indeed quite naturally from the pardoning father-love of God. Now the thought of the ransom (Mk. 10:45) recalls the Pauline theory of the atonement with its juridical character. This, indeed, has reference to the forgiveness of sins. It is therefore to be presumed that the juridical notion of the atonement, like the thought of the forgiveness of sins, was strange to Jesus, since it is not suggested by anything in the whole character of his teaching. Consequently the expressions about the significance of his Passion are in their traditional form influenced somehow or another by Pauline conceptions.

If one takes due account of this influence, the historical saying (Mk. 10:45) contains the notion of serving through sacrifice. This thought is here expressed in its highest potency. We stand upon the border where the heightened conception of service leads to that of sacrifice and atonement. The value of this sacrifice for others consists in the fact that this suffering death which Jesus underwent is at the same time the inaugural act through which the new morality of the Kingdom of God receives emphatic sanction and the new condition contemplated in the idea of the Kingdom is itself realised. This deed is the efficient first factor in a chain of transformations the supernatural conclusion of which is his "coming again" in glory, where the New Covenant which he sealed with his blood is fulfilled in him.

Therewith it is also explained why the determination to encounter suffering and death could and must suggest itself. The realisation of the Kingdom of God was Jesus' mission. This he had undertaken to effect at first within narrow limits during his Galilean ministry. Through his preaching of the new morality grounded upon faith in the divine Father, and under the influence of the power which proceeded from him, the beginnings of this Kingdom developed. It was a happy, successful period—the "Galilean spring time," Keim called it. The climax of this period was reached with the mission of the Disciples. Through their preaching the glorious seed was to be strewn abroad everywhere. As they upon their return announced to him their success he broke out with the cry of exultation which accounted the victory already present (Mt. 11:25–27).

Then came the time of defeat. The opposition was contrived and carried out from Jerusalem (Mk. 7:1). Before this the sympathy of the people delivered him from the consequences of occasional friction with the officials. Now, however, as the opposition was systematically pursued, even his followers fell away from him. It was ominous that the discussion about ceremonial purification brought to light the contradiction in which Jesus found himself with the legal tradition (Mk. 7:1–23). Before spring had again returned to the land he had been obliged to leave Galilee. Far away in the north, in quiet and solitary retirement, he collected his energies in the effort perfectly to understand himself.

For the realisation of the Kingdom there remained but one way still open to him,—namely, conflict with the power which opposed his work. He resolved to carry this conflict into the capital itself. There fate should decide. Perhaps the victory would fall to him. But, even if it should turn out that in the course of earthly events the fate of death awaited him inevitably, so long as he trod the path which his office prescribed, this very suffering of death must signify in God's plan the performance by which his work was to be crowned. It was then God's will that the moral state appropriate to the Kingdom of God should be inaugurated by the highest moral deed of the Messiah. With this thought he set out for Jerusalem—in order to remain Messiah.

2. *The Four Assumptions of the Modern-Historical Solution*

1. The life of Jesus falls into two contrasted epochs. The first was fortunate, the second brought disillusion and ill success.

2. The form of the Synoptical Passion-idea in Mk. 10:45 (his giving himself a ransom for many) and in the institution of the Lord's Supper (Mk. 14:24: his blood given for many) is somehow or another influenced by the Pauline theory of the atonement.

3. The conception of the Kingdom of God as a self-fulfilling ethical society in which service is the highest law dominated the idea of the Passion.

4. If Jesus' Passion was the inaugural act of the new morality of the Kingdom of God, the success of it depended upon the Disciples being led to understand it in this sense and to act in accordance with it. The Passion-idea was a reflection.

Are these assumptions, considered individually, justified?

3. *The Two Contrasted Periods* (First Assumption)

The period of ill success is dated from the time following the mission of the Twelve. What are the events of the supposedly fortunate period? We pass over the vexatious discussion with the Pharisees about the healing of the paralytic (Mk. 2:1–12), over the question of fasting (Mk. 2:18–22), and that of the observance of the Sabbath (Mk. 2:23–3:6). Already in Mk. 3:6 it has come to the point of a murderous attack. Jesus has to renounce his family because they wish to fetch him home by force as one who is mentally incompetent (Mk. 3:20–22,31–35). At Nazareth he is rejected (Mk. 6:1–6).

In the same period occurs the attack which shocked him

most profoundly. The Pharisees discredited him with the people by charging that he was in league with the devil (Mk. 3:22–30). How deeply this saying wounded him may be seen from his reference to it in the commission to the Twelve. He prepared his Disciples for a similar experience. "If they have called the master of the house Beelzebub, how much more those of his household" (Mt. 10:25).

Such are the well known events of the "successful period"! But they are nothing in comparison with those which he hints at when he is sending out the Twelve. In general terms he has already pronounced those blessed who are reproached and persecuted for his sake (Mt. 5:11, 12). Now he leads his Disciples to expect oppression and distress (Mt. 10:17–25). Faithfulness to him involves the endurance of enmity (Mt. 10:22), the severance of the dearest ties (Mt. 10:37), and the bearing of the cross (Mt. 10:38). The Galilean period is to be regarded as a *happy* one: the commission to the Twelve is *pessimistic* in tone. How does that agree?

The hints also which he drops at that time in the presence of the people point to bitter catastrophes. What must have occurred in Chorazin, in Capernaum, and in Bethsaida that he calls down upon them the wrath of the Day of Judgment, in which it shall be more tolerable for Tyre and Sidon than for them (Mt. 11:20–24)!

Because this gloomy tone accords ill with the happy Galilean period, there is an obvious temptation to regard the Matthean speeches of the time of the Apostles' mission as compositions which include fragments belonging to a later period. Where, however, could Jesus have spoken such words? So long as he remained in the north after the flight he made no speeches, and the utterances of the Jerusalem days have their own peculiar character, so that it is hard to know where to introduce references to Galilean occurrences and warnings to the Disciples in prospect of their journey.

Moreover, it is a fact that nothing is related about conspicuous successes in the first period. The successes first begin with the mission of the Twelve. Jesus celebrates the great moment of their return with words of enthusiasm (Mt. 11:25–27). Are we to suppose now that in the sequel the Pharisees triumphed over him completely and the people deserted him? Of such a retrogression of his cause the texts, however, record nothing. The discussion about ceremonial purification (Mt. 7:1–23) does not furnish what was expected of it. Jesus had already at an earlier time come into much hotter conflict with the theologians of the capital (Mk. 3:22–30). In the question about the laws of purification it was not he that was worsted.

Jesus' defeat has been inferred from the fact that the "flight" to the north followed this scene (Mk. 7:24 ff). But the accounts do not in the least represent this departure as a flight, nor do they account for this journey to the north as a result of the previous controversy; rather it is *we* who interpolate a fictitious causal connection in the chronological sequence of the narrative. If Jesus immediately before this was supported by the popular favour and now leaves the region, we have a fact before us which stands unexplained in the texts. That it was a flight is an unprovable conjecture.

No importance need be attached to the fact that subsequently Jesus again appears on two occasions surrounded by a multitude (Mk. 8:1–9: feeding of the 4000; and Mk. 8:34 ff: the scenes before and after the Transfiguration). This fact might perhaps be attributed to a literary reconstruction of the respective accounts,—as may be considered established, for example, in the case of the *doublette* of the feeding of the multitude.

Decisive, however, is the reception which the Passover caravan accorded to Jesus as he overtook it at Jericho. This ovation was not accorded to the man who had lost ground before the Pharisees in his own country and among his own people and at last had been forced to flee, but to the celebrated prophet emerging from his retirement. If this Galilean populace supported him now by their acclaim and enabled him to terrorise the magistrates in the capital for several days—for his purification of the Temple was nothing else but that—and to expose the scribes with his dry irony, is it possible that they did it for the man who a few weeks before had to yield to these theologians in his own land?

If one insists upon speaking of a successful period, it is the *second* that must be so denominated. For wherever Jesus appears in public after the return of the Twelve he is accompanied by a devoted multitude—in Galilee, from the Jordan to Jerusalem, and in the capital itself. The surly Jewish populace is an invention of the Fourth Evangelist. Then, too, the illegality of his secret arrest and hasty conviction shows what the Council feared from the popular favour in behalf of Jesus. That was the only "ill success" of the second period. It was indeed a fatal one.

The first and successful Galilean period is therefore in reality a time of humiliation and ill success. There is a double reason for regarding it nevertheless as a "happy" time. In the first place there is an æsthetic element in it, which Keim in particular strongly emphasises. A series of parables drawn from nature, as well as the wonderful speech against worldly care (Mt. 6:25–34), seem hardly intelligible except as the reflection of a glad and cheerful sense for the beauty of nature.

With this is associated, in the second place, an *historical postulate.* In the first period no trace is discoverable of the idea of the Passion: the second is dominated by it. Hence the first was successful, the second unsuccessful,—for otherwise there is no way of accounting, psychologically or historically, for the change.

The historical facts speak differently. In the real period of ill success the resolution to suffer did not come to light. In the successful second period, on the other hand, Jesus disclosed to his Disciples that he must be put to death by the scribes. Thus the relation was the reverse. Herewith modern-historical psychology finds itself before an enigma.

4. *The Influence of the Pauline Theory of the Atonement upon the Formulation of the Synoptical Prediction of the Passion* (Second Assumption)

No proof can be brought to support the contention that the Passion passages in the Synoptic Gospels are influenced by Pauline conceptions. Here again we have a sort of postulate. For if the juridical character of Mk. 10:45 and Mk. 14:24 cannot be set down to the account of the Pauline medium, one must assume that Jesus' own notion of the Passion contained this bold conception of atonement. The modern-historical solution, however, is not adapted to that alternative.

As a matter of fact it is demonstrable that no Pauline influence can be discerned here. According to Paul, Jesus said at the Last Supper: My body for *you* (I Cor. 11:24). In the same manner Luke has: My body which is given for *you;* the blood which is shed for *you* (Lk. 22:19, 20). Both the older Synoptists invariably write instead of this:

for *many*. Mk. 10:45; Mt. 20:28: to give his life a ransom for *many*. Mk. 14:24; Mt. 26:28: my blood of the covenant which is shed for *many*. In the one case the persons who are to benefit by the Passion are definitely determined: they are the Disciples. In the other case it is a question of an indefinite number.

Nothing is accomplished by the argument that it comes in the end substantially to the same thing. Why, according to the older Synoptists, did Jesus speak of the *many*, according to Paul, of *his own*? The sole explanation lies in the fact that Paul wrote from the standpoint of the Church after the death of Jesus. From this point of view the saving efficacy of Jesus' death is applied to a determinate community, to those, namely, who believe on him. The Disciples represent this community of believers in the historical sayings of Jesus, because from the standpoint of the Church, founded as it was upon belief in the Messiah, one could not conceive that Jesus' words about his Passion could have any other reference but to the believers.

The early Synoptic "for many" is uttered, however, from the *historical standpoint*. That is to say, it is appropriate to the time when Jesus did not yet require belief in his messiahship, when consequently the number of persons whom his death is to benefit is left indeterminate. Of only one thing is he certain, that it is greater than the circle of his Disciples: hence he said, "for many." Had he used the expression, "for you," which Paul thought it natural to attribute to him, the Disciples must have concluded from it that he was dying for them alone, inasmuch as they could not then have the feeling that they were representatives of a future community of believers, according to the conception which was so obvious to Paul and the Church.

Inasmuch as this *"for many"* has held its place, in spite of the fact that Paul, writing from the churchly point of view, felt instinctively the necessity of substituting *"for you"* (though he thereby coined an expression which is historically impossible), one is not justified in assuming any sort of Pauline influence upon the traditional form of the early Synoptic Passion-idea. The bold theory of the atonement in the Synoptists is therefore historical. Any softening of it, such as the modern-historical solution must assume, is without justification.

Hence in the interpretation of Jesus' saying the first requisite is to do justice to the expression "for many." Because they have not done this, all expositions of the significance of Jesus' death—from Paul to Ritschl—are unhistorical. One has but to substitute, for the community of believers with which they deal, the indeterminate and unqualified "many" of the historical saying, and their interpretation become simply meaningless. That interpretation alone is historical which renders it intelligible why, according to Jesus, the atonement accomplished by his death is to redound to the benefit of a number which is intentionally left indeterminate.

5. *The Kingdom of God as an Ethical Entity in the Passion Idea* (Third Assumption)

(*a*) Mk. 10:41–45. Service as the ethical conduct prescribed in expectation of the coming Kingdom.

The sons of Zebedee had advanced the claim to sit on either side of the Lord in his glory, i.e. when he should reign as Messiah upon his throne. The other Disciples object to this. Jesus calls them together and speaks to them about serving and ruling in connection with the Kingdom of God.

In this saying one is accustomed to find the ethical conception of the Kingdom of God. There is to be a revaluation of all values. The greatest in the Kingdom of heaven is he who becomes least, like a child (Mt. 18:4), and the ruler is he who serves. Self-humiliation and the meekness of service, such is the new morality of the Kingdom of God which comes into force through Jesus' service unto death.

With this, however, the fact is ignored that the Kingdom in which one reigns is thought of as a future thing, whereas the serving applies to the present! In our ethical fashion of viewing the matter, serving and reigning coincide logically and chronologically. With Jesus, however, it is not at all a question of a purely ethical exchange of the notions of serving and ruling; rather it is a contrast which develops in a chronological sequence. There is a sharp distinction made between the present and the future æon. He who is one day to count among the greatest in the Kingdom of God must *now* be as a child! He who advances a claim to a position of rule therein must *now* serve! The more lowly the position of humble service which one *now* assumes, in the time when the earthly rulers exercise authority by force, so much the more lofty will be his station as ruler when earthly force is done away and the Kingdom of God dawns. Hence he especially must humble himself even unto death who is to come as the Son of Man upon the clouds of heaven to judge and to rule the world. Before he mounts his throne he drinks the cup of suffering, which they also must taste who would reign with him!

So soon as one pays due attention to this "now and then" in Jesus' speech, the trivial parallelism of phrase is replaced by a real and effective climax. The descending stages of service correspond to the ascending stages of rule.

1. Whosoever would become great *among you,* shall be *your* servant—Mk. 10:43.

2. Whosoever of *you* would be first, shall be bond-servant of *all* (others)—v. 44.

3. Therefore the Son of Man expected the post of highest rule because he was not come to be served but to serve, in giving his life a ransom for *many*—v. 45.

The climax is a double one. The service of the Disciples extended only to *their* circle: the service of Jesus to an unlimited number, namely, to all such as were to benefit by his suffering and death. In the case of the Disciples it was merely a question of unselfish *subjection:* in the case of Jesus it meant the bitter *suffering of death.* Both count as serving, inasmuch as they establish a claim to a position of rule in the Kingdom.

The ordinary explanation does not satisfy the early Synoptic text but only that of Luke 22:24–27. This text has torn the narrative from its proper connection, so that it appears as a dispute among the Disciples "which of them is accounted to be the greatest."

With this, the "now and then" is eliminated from the situation, and it is only a question of a purely ethical inversion of the ideas of ruling and serving. Accordingly, Jesus' speech, too, runs on in a lifeless parallelism. He that is greater among you, let him become as the younger, and he that is chief, as he that doth serve (Lk. 22:26). Instead of exemplifying by his own sacrifice of himself unto death for the great generality of men the conduct required of those who would reign with him, he speaks only of his serviceable character as displayed towards the Disciples: But I am in the midst of you as he that serveth (Lk. 22:27). By this he means a serving that is at the same time ruling. In the case of the two older Synoptists, however, it is not at all a question of the proclamation of the new morality of the Kingdom of God, where serving is ruling; rather it is a question of the significance of humility and service in *expectation of the Kingdom of God.* Service is the fundamental law of *interim-ethics*.

This thought is much deeper and more vital than the modern play upon words which we attribute to the Lord. Only through lowliness and childlikeness in this æon is one worthily prepared to reign in the Kingdom of God. Only he who is here morally purified and ennobled through suffering can be great there. Hence suffering is for Jesus the moral means of acquiring and confirming the messianic authority to which he is designated.

Earthly rule, because it depends upon force, is an emanation of the power of ungodliness. Authority in the Kingdom of God, where the power of this world is destroyed, signifies emanation from the divine power. Only he can be the bearer of such authority who has kept himself free from the contamination of earthly rule. To allot it to such as have prepared themselves through suffering is God's affair and his alone (Mk. 10:39, 40).

But if service does not represent the morality of the Kingdom of God, Jesus' conception of the Passion does not deal with the corresponding notion of the Kingdom as a self-developing ethical society, but rather with a super-moral entity, namely, the Kingdom of God in its eschatological aspect.

(*b*) The idea of the Passion and the Eschatological Expectation.

The investigation of the accounts of the Lord's Supper [in the first part of this work] revealed a close connection between the eschatological conclusion (Mk. 14:25) and the expression about the blood shed for many (v. 25). The other passages about the Passion suggest a similar connection.

After Jesus with his "Yes" had himself pronounced the verdict of death he speaks of his "coming again" upon the clouds of heaven. Hereby, according to Mark's text, he associates the two events in a single thought. Mk. 14:62: I am, and ye shall see the Son of Man sitting at the right hand of the Power and coming with the clouds of Heaven. This logical connection is already weakened by Matthew, as in the case of the word about the cup. He substitutes for the "and" an expression which denotes a temporal sequence merely. Mt. 26:64: Thou hast said: *nevertheless* I say unto you, *henceforth* shall ye, etc. The eschatological reference is lacking in Luke: he has omitted it also from the word about the cup.

A close connection between the thought of the Passion and eschatology is implied also in Jesus' saying about the path of suffering which his followers must tread (Mk. 8:34–9:1). Whosoever shall be ashamed of Jesus when he suffers reproach and persecution in this adulterous and sinful world, of him will the Son of Man be ashamed when he cometh in the glory of his Father with the holy angels. For this generation shall not sink into the grave until they see the Kingdom of God come with power!

This connection must have appeared extremely prominent to the hearers. After the departure from Cæsarea Philippi, under the impression of the secret of the Passion, which filled them with a sense of sadness and fear (Mk. 9:30–32),—the Disciples dispute which of them shall receive the highest place in the Kingdom. In the house at Capernaum Jesus had to rebuke them (Mk. 9:33–37). That was after he had spoken for the second time about his Passion.

On the way to Jerusalem the same scene was reënacted in closest conjunction with the third prediction of the Passion (Mk. 10:32–41). The sons of Zebedee advance their claim to the seats upon the throne. This is not in the least a case of childish misunderstanding on the part of his followers, for Jesus in fact treats their suggestion with perfect seriousness. The eschatological expectation must accordingly have been thrown into such strong relief for the Disciples by Jesus' prediction of his Passion that they necessarily reasoned within themselves about the position they should occupy in the coming Kingdom.

The modern-historical solution eliminates the eschatological conception of the Kingdom of God from the Passion, reducing it to the notion of an apotheosis, "the coming *again,*" as it is called. This expression is entirely false. Jesus never spoke of his coming *again* but only of his *coming* or the *advent* of the Son of Man. We use the expression "coming again" because we connect death and glory by contrast, as though the new situation were conditioned merely upon a victorious transfiguration of Jesus. Our view makes him say: "I shall die, but I shall be glorified through my coming again." As a matter of fact, however, he said: "I must suffer *and* the Son of Man shall appear upon the clouds of heaven." But that for his hearers meant much more than an apotheosis—for with the appearing of the Son of Man dawned the eschatological Kingdom. Jesus therefore sets his death in temporal-causal connection with the eschatological dawning of the Kingdom. The *eschatological* notion of the Kingdom, not the *modern-ethical* notion, dominates his idea of the Passion.

6. *The Form of the Prediction of the Passion*
(Fourth Assumption)

If the modern historical solution be correct in its conception, Jesus must have communicated the thought of the Passion to his Disciples in the form of an ethical *re-*

flection. If they were to comprehend the approaching catastrophe as the inauguration of the new morality, and were to derive from it incentive to a change of conduct, then he must have familiarised them with the character of this event from the very beginning, as soon as ever he announced it.

As a matter of fact, however, he imparted to them the thought of the Passion, not in the form of an *ethical reflection,* but as a *secret,* without further explanation. It is dominated by a "must," the expression for incomprehensible divine necessity. The fact that the Passion idea was a secret stands opposed to the modern-historical solution.

7. *Résumé*

1. The assumption of a fortunate Galilean period which was followed by a time of defeat is historically untenable.

2. Pauline influence cannot have conditioned the form of the early Synoptic sayings about the Passion.

3. Not the ethical but the hyper-ethical, the eschatological, notion of the Kingdom dominates the Passion as Jesus conceived it.

4. The utterances of the Passion-idea did not occur in the form of an ethical reflection but it was a question of an incomprehensible secret which the Disciples had not the least need to understand and in fact did not.

Such is the situation with regard to the four pillars of the modern-historical solution. With them the whole structure collapses. It is after all a lifeless thought! The feeble modernity of it is visible in the fact that it does not get beyond a sort of representative significance of Jesus' death. Jesus effects by his offering of himself nothing absolutely new, since throughout his whole public ministry he assumes that the Kingdom of God is already present as a dispensation of the forgiveness of sin or as the morally developing society. With his very appearance upon earth it is there. The performance of atonement, however, requires a *real* significance in Jesus' death.

Herein lies the weakness of the modern dogmatic in contrast with the old. Paul, Anselm, and Luther know of an absolutely new situation which follows in time the death of Jesus and results as a consequence of it. Modern theology talks all around the subject; it has nothing specific to say, however, but involves itself in the cloud of its own assumptions. Both accounts, indeed, are unhistorical. Religiously considered, only the modern view is justifiable. The old dogmatic, however, is in this point the more historical, for it postulates at all events a real effect of the death of Jesus, as the Synoptical passages require.

In what, however, does this absolutely new thing consist which is there made to depend upon the death of Jesus? The Synoptic sayings give but one answer to this: the eschatological realisation of the Kingdom! The coming of the Kingdom of God with power is dependent upon the atonement which Jesus performs. That is substantially the secret of the Passion.

How is that to be understood? Only the history of Jesus can throw light upon it. *In place of the modern-historical solution we advance now the eschatological-historical.*

CHAPTER II

The "Development" of Jesus

1. *The Kingdom of God as an Ethical and as an Eschatological Fact*

The concurrence in Jesus of an ethical with an eschatological line of thought has always constituted one of the most difficult problems of New Testament study. How can two such different views of the world, in part diametrically opposed to one another, be united in *one* process of thought?

The attempt has been made to evade the problem, with the just feeling that the two views cannot be united. Critical spirits like T. Colani (*Jesus-Christ et les croyances messianiques de son temps.* 1864, pp. 94 ff, 169 ff) and G. Volkmar (*Die Evangelien.* 1870, pp. 530 ff) went to the length of eliminating altogether eschatology from the field of Jesus' thought. All expressions of that sort were accordingly to be charged to the account of the eschatological expectation of a later time. This procedure is frustrated by the stubbornness of the texts: the eschatological sayings belong precisely to the best attested passages. The excision of them is an act of violence.

No more successful has been the attempt to evade the problem by *sublimating* the eschatology, as though Jesus had translated the realistic conceptions of his time into spiritual terms by using them in a figurative sense. The work of Eric Haupt (*Die eschatologischen Aussagen Jesu in den synoptischen Evangelien,* 1895) is based upon this thought. But there is nothing to justify us in assuming that Jesus attached to his words a non-natural sense, whereas his hearers, in accordance with the prevailing view, must have understood them realistically. Not only are we at a loss for a rational explanation of such a method on Jesus' part, but he himself gives not the slightest hint of it.

So the problem remains as urgent as ever, how the juxtaposition of two discordant views of the world is to be explained. The sole solution seems to lie in the assumption of a gradual development. Jesus may have entertained at first a purely ethical view, looking for the realisation of the Kingdom of God through the spread and perfection of the moral-religious society which he was undertaking to establish. When, however, the opposition of the world put the organic completion of the Kingdom in doubt, the eschatological conception forced itself upon him. By the course of events he was brought to the pass where the fulfilment of the religious-ethical ideal, which hitherto he had regarded as the terminus of a continuous moral development, could be expected only as the result of a cosmic catastrophe in which God's omnipotence should bring to its conclusion the work which he had undertaken.

Thus a complete revolution is supposed to have occurred in Jesus' thought. But the problem is veiled rather than solved by disposing the terms of the contrast in chronological sequence. The acceptance of the eschatological notion, if it is to be rendered intelligible in this fashion, signifies nothing less than a total breach with the past, a break at which all development ceases. For the eschatological thought, if it be taken seriously, abrogates the ethical train of thought. It accepts no subordinate place. To such a position of impotence it was brought for the first time in Christian theology as the result of historical experience. Jesus, however, must have thought either eschatologically or uneschatologically, but not both together—nor in such a wise that the eschatological was superadded to supplement the uneschatological.

It has been proved that in the thought of the Passion it is only the eschatological idea of the Kingdom of God which is in view. It has been shown likewise that the assumption of a period of ill success after the mission of the Twelve is without historical justification. This, however, constitutes the indispensable presumption for every such development as has been assumed on the part of Jesus. Therefore the eschatological notion cannot have been forced upon Jesus by outward experiences, but it must from the beginning, even in the first Galilean period, have lain at the base of his preaching!

2. *The Eschatological Character of the Charge to the Twelve*

"The Kingdom of God is at hand" (Mt. 10:7)—this word which Jesus commissions his Disciples to proclaim is a summary expression of all his previous preaching. They are to carry it now throughout the cities of Israel. The charge of Jesus to the Twelve furnishes no means of determining in what sense this proclamation is meant.

If the common conception is right about the significance of this mission of the Twelve, the words with which he dismisses them present an extraordinary riddle. Full of hope and with the joy of productive effort he goes about to extend the scope of his activity for the founding of the Kingdom of God. The commission to the Twelve ought therefore to contain instruction about the missionary propaganda they were to carry out in this sense. One must hence expect that he would direct them how they should preach about the new relation to God and the new morality of the Kingdom.

The commission, however, is anything but a summary of the "teaching of Jesus." It does not in the least contemplate instruction of a thoroughgoing kind, rather what is in question is a flying proclamation throughout Israel. The one errand of the Apostles as teachers is to cry out everywhere the warning of the nearness of the Kingdom of God—to the intent that all may be warned and given opportunity to repent. In this, however, no time is to be lost; therefore they are not to linger in a town where men are unsusceptible to their message, but to hasten on in order that they may pass through all the cities of Israel before the appearing of the Son of Man takes place. But "the coming of the Son of Man" signifies—*the dawning of the Kingdom of God with power.*

When they persecute you in this city flee unto another, for verily I say unto you, Ye shall not have gone through the cities of Israel till the Son of Man be come (Mt. 10:23). If one so understands the commission to the Twelve as to suppose that Jesus would say through his Disciples that the time is now come for the realisation of the Kingdom by a new moral behaviour, that eschatological saying lies like an erratic boulder in the midst of a flowery meadow. If, however, one conceives of the embassage eschatologically, the saying acquires a great context: it is a rock in the midst of a wild mountain landscape. One cannot affirm of this saying that it has been interpolated here by a later age; rather with compelling force it fixes the presence of eschatological conceptions in the days of the mission of the Twelve.

The one and only article of instruction that is required is the call to repentance. Whosoever believes in the nearness of the Kingdom, repents. Hence Jesus gives the Disciples authority over unclean spirits, to cast them out and to heal the sick (Mt. 10:1). By these signs they are to perceive that the power of ungodliness is coming to an end and the morning-glow of the Kingdom of God already dawns. That belongs to their errand as teachers, for whosoever fails to believe their signs, and thereupon brings forth no works of repentance unto the Kingdom of God,—that man is damned. Thus have Chorazin, Bethsaida, and Capernaum come into condemnation. Faith and repentance were made easy for them by the signs and wonders with which they were favoured beyond others—and yet they did not come to themselves, as even pagan cities like Tyre and Sidon would have done (Mt. 11:20–24). This saying addressed to the people shows what significance Jesus ascribed to the signs in view of the eschatological embassage.

Thus the Disciples were to preach *the Kingdom, Repentance, and the Judgment.* Inasmuch, however, as the event they proclaimed was so near that it might at any moment surprise them, they must be prepared for what precedes it, namely, for the final insurrection of the power of this world. How they are to comport themselves in the face of this emergency so as not to be confounded—here is the point upon which Jesus' parting words of instruction bear! In the general tumult of spirits all ties will be dissolved. Faction will divide even the family (Mt. 10:34–36). Whosoever would be loyal to the Kingdom of God must be ready to tear from out his heart those who were dearest to him, to endure reproach, and to bear the cross (Mt. 10:37, 38). The secular authority will bring upon them severe persecution (Mt. 10:17, 31). Men will call them to account and subject them to torture in order to move them to denial of their cause. Brother shall deliver up brother to death, and the father his child; and children shall rise up against parents and cause them to be put to death. Only he who remains steadfast in the midst of this general tumult, and confesses Jesus before men, shall be saved in the Day of Judgment, when he intervenes with God in their behalf (Mt. 10:32, 33).

In the commission to the Twelve Jesus imparts instruction about the woes of the approaching Kingdom. In the descriptive portions of it there may be much perhaps that betrays the colouring of a later time. By this concession, however, the character of the speech as a whole is not prejudiced. The question at issue is not about a course of conduct which they are to maintain *after his death.* For such instruction not a single historical word can be adduced. The woes precede the dawning of the Kingdom. Therefore the victorious proclamation of the nearness of the Kingdom must accommodate itself to the woes. Hence this juxtaposition of optimism and pessimism which the current interpretation finds so unaccountable. It is the sign manual of every eschatological *Weltanschauung.*

3. *The New View*

The idea of Passion is dominated *only* by the eschatological conception of the Kingdom. In the charge to the Twelve the question is *only* about the eschatological—not about the ethical-nearness of the Kingdom. From this it follows, for one thing, that Jesus' ministry counted *only* upon the eschatological realisation of the Kingdom. Then, however, it is evident that the relation of his ethical thoughts to the eschatological view can have suffered no alteration by reason of outward events but must have been the same from beginning to end.

In what relation, however, did his ethics and his eschatology stand to each other? So long as one starts with the ethics and seeks to comprehend the eschatology as something adventitious, there appears to be no organic connection between the two, since the ethics of Jesus, as we are accustomed to conceive it, is not in the least accommodated to the eschatology but stands upon a much higher level. One must therefore take the opposite course and see if the ethical proclamation in essence is not conditioned by the eschatological view of the world.

CHAPTER III

The Preaching of the Kingdom of God

1. *The New Morality as Repentance*

If the thought of the eschatological realisation of the Kingdom is the fundamental factor in Jesus' preaching, his whole theory of ethics must come under the conception of *repentance* as a preparation for the coming of the Kingdom. This conception seems to us too narrow a one to apply to the whole extent of this moral-religious proclamation. This is due to the fact that the word repentance as we use it has rather a negative significance, laying emphasis as it does chiefly upon foregoing guilt. It is a far richer conception, however, which the Synoptists express by the word repentance (μετάνοια). It is not merely a recovery which stands in retrospective relation with a sinful condition in the past, but also—and this is its predominant character—*it is a moral renewal in prospect of the accomplishment of universal perfection in the future.*

Thus "the repentance in expectation of the Kingdom" comprises all positive ethical requirements. In this sense it is the lively echo of the "repentance" of the early prophets. For what Amos, Hosea, Isaiah, and Jeremiah mean by repentance is moral renovation in prospect of the Day of the Lord. Thus Isaiah says: "Wash you, make you clean; put away the evil of your doings from before mine eyes; seek judgment, relieve the oppressed, judge the fatherless, plead for the widow" (Isai. 1:16, 17). It is precisely this Old Testament conception of repentance, with its emphasis upon the new moral life, which one must have in mind in order to understand aright the Synoptical repentance. Both have a forward vision, both are dominated by the thought of a condition of perfection which God will bring to pass through the Judgment. This, in the Prophetic view, is the Day of the Lord; in the Synoptic it is the dawn of the Kingdom.

The ethics of the Sermon on the Mount is therefore repentance. The new morality, which detects the spirit beneath the letter of the Law, makes one meet for the Kingdom of God. Only the righteous can enter into the Kingdom of God—in that conviction all were agreed. Whosoever, therefore, preached the nearness of the Kingdom must also teach the righteousness pertaining to the Kingdom. Hence Jesus proclaimed the new righteousness which is higher than the Law and the Prophets,—for they extend only up to the Baptist. Since the days of the Baptist, however, one stands immediately within the premessianic period.

The Day of Judgment puts this moral transformation to the proof: only he who has done the will of the heavenly Father can enter into the Kingdom (Mt. 7:21). The claim that one is a follower of Jesus, or has even wrought signs and wonders in his name, is of no avail as a substitute for this new righteousness (Mt. 7:22, 23). Hence the Sermon on the Mount concludes with the admonition to build, in expectation of the momentous event, a firmly founded structure capable of resisting storm and tempest (Mt. 7:24–27).

The Beatitudes (Mt. 5:3–12) come under the same point of view. They define the moral disposition which justifies admission into the Kingdom. This is the explanation of the use of the present and the future tense in the same sentence. Blessed are the meek, those that hunger and thirst after righteousness, the merciful, the pure in heart, the peacemakers, the poor in spirit, those that endure persecution for righteousness' sake, because such character and conduct is their security that with the appearing of the Kingdom of God they will be found to belong to it.

A series of parables illustrates the same thought. Thus the parables of the treasure in the field and of the pearl of great price (Mt. 13:44–46) show how one must stake all upon the hope of the Kingdom when the prospect of it is held out to him, and must sacrifice all other goods for the sake of acquiring this highest good that is proposed to him.

Thus already in the ethics of the Galilean period we find the "now and then" which accounts for the estimate put upon serving (Mk. 10:45). *As repentance unto the Kingdom of God the ethics also of the Sermon on the Mount is interim-ethics.* In this we perceive that the moral instruction of Jesus remained the same from the first day of his public appearance unto his latest utterances, for the lowliness and serviceableness which he recommended to his Disciples on the way to Jerusalem correspond exactly to the new moral conduct which he developed in the Sermon on the Mount: they make one meet for the Kingdom of God. Only, they constitute a climax in the attainment of the new righteousness, inasmuch as they render one meet not merely for entrance into the Kingdom but for bearing rule in it.

We encounter again the *Leitmotiv* of the Sermon on the Mount in the epilogue to the great parables uttered in Jerusalem. Nothing but the maintenance of the new morality in all relations of life guarantees entrance into the Kingdom. Hence Jesus can say to the Pharisee who agrees to the summary of this new morality as it is expressed in the commandment of love: Thou art not far from the Kingdom of God (Mk. 12:34). That does not mean that the Pharisee by such a disposition of mind has already well nigh risen to the height of the "morality of the Kingdom." For if the double commandment of love constituted the morality of the *Kingdom,* Jesus must have said to him (since he entirely agreed to these commandments): Thou belongest to the Kingdom. The "not far" must in fact be understood in a purely chronological sense, not as denoting some small measure of perfection which the man still lacks. He is not far from the Kingdom of God because he possesses the moral quality which will identify him as a member of the same when after a short space it appears. The "not far" contains therefore the same mixture of present and future tense which we have remarked in the Beatitudes.

Reasoning from our ethical point of view we are inclined to apply the conception of reward to this relation between membership in the Kingdom and the new morality. This, however, does not completely render the thought of Jesus, which had to do above all with the *immediateness* of the transition from the condition of moral renewal into the super-moral perfection of the Kingdom of God. Whosoever at the dawning of the Kingdom is in possession of a character morally renovated, he will be found a member of the same. This is the adequate expression for the relation of morality to the coming Kingdom of God.

2. *The Ethics of Jesus and Modern Ethics*

The depth of Jesus' religious ethics encourages us to expect that we can find our own modern-ethical consciousness reflected in it. With respect to its eternal inward truth it is indeed independent of history and unconditioned by it, since it already contains the highest ethical thoughts of all times. Nevertheless there exists a great difference between Jesus' sentiment and ours. Modern ethics is "unconditional," since it creates of itself the new ethical situation,—the presumption being that this situation will evolve unto final perfection. Ethics is here an end in itself, inasmuch as the moral perfection of mankind comes to the same thing as the perfection of the Kingdom of God. That is Kant's thought. This self-sufficiency of ethics (which however, exacts a certain resignation in view of the distant consummation) shows that the modern-Christian theory is permeated by Hellenistic-rationalistic ideas and has undergone a development of two millenniums.

The ethics of Jesus on the other hand is "conditional," in the sense that it stands in indissoluble connection with the expectation of a state of perfection which is to be supernaturally brought about. Thereby its Jewish origin is revealed, and its immediate connection with the Prophetic ethics, in which the moral conduct of the people was conditioned by a definite expectation. Hence, if any parallel at all may be adduced in explanation of the ethics of Jesus, it can be only the Prophetic, never the modern. For in proportion as the latter enters into it the mode of conception becomes unhistorical, Jesus' ethics being treated as self-sufficient, whereas in fact it is oriented entirely by the expected supernatural consummation.

So there has been created the insoluble problem, that a person thoroughly modern so far as his ethics is concerned should incidentally give utterance to eschatological expressions. But if we once perceive the conditional character of Jesus' ethics, and seriously consider its connection with the ethics of the Prophets, it is immediately clear that all conceptions of the Kingdom as a growth out of small beginnings, all notions about an ethics of the Kingdom, or about the development of it, have been foisted upon Jesus by our modern consciousness—simply because we could not readily familiarise ourselves with the thought that the ethics of Jesus is conditional.

We make him conceive of the Kingdom of God as if its historical realisation represented a narrow opening through which it had to squeeze before attaining the full stature which belongs to it. That is a modern conception. For Jesus and the Prophets, however, it was a thing impossible. In the immediateness of their ethical view there is no place for a morality of the Kingdom of God or for a development of the Kingdom—it lies beyond the borders of good and evil; it will be brought about by a cosmic catastrophe through which evil is to be completely overcome. Hence all moral criteria are to be abolished. *The Kingdom of God is super-moral.*

To this height of hyper-ethical idealism the modern consciousness is no longer capable of soaring. History has aged us too much for that. But for the historical understanding of the ethics of Jesus it is the indispensable assumption.

In addition to this, when we think of the Kingdom, our thought stretches forward to the coming generations which are to realise it in ever increasing measure. Jesus' glance is directed backward. For him the Kingdom is composed of the generations which have already gone down to the grave and which are now to be awakened unto a state of perfection. How should there be for him any ethics of sexual relations, when he explains to the Sadducees that in the Kingdom of God after the great Resurrection there will be no longer any sexual relations at all, "but they will be like the angels of heaven" (Mk. 10:25)?

Every ethical form of Jesus, be it never so perfect, leads therefore only up to the frontier of the Kingdom of

God, while every trace of a path disappears so soon as one advances upon the new territory. There one needs it no more.

We have a prejudice against this conception of conditional ethics. It is an unjustified prejudice if it is due to a suspicion that Jesus' ethics is thereby disparaged. Exactly the opposite is the case. For this conditionality springs from an absolute ethical idealism, which postulates for the expected state of perfection conditions of existence which are themselves ethical. In our unconditional and self-sufficing ethics we, however, assume that the conflict between good and evil must go on forever, as belonging constantly to the nature of the ethical. Ethics and theology do not stand for us in the same lively relationship as they do with Jesus. The vividness of the colours of the absolute ethical idealism has been faded by history. So, to render the ethics of Jesus unconditional and self-sufficing is not only unhistorical, but it means also the degradation of his ethical idealism.

On one point, however, our ethical sentiment is justified in its prejudice. If ethics has to do only with the expectation of the supernatural consummation, its actual worth is diminished, since it is merely individual ethics and is concerned only with the relation of each single person to the Kingdom of God. The thought, however, that the moral community which has been constituted by Jesus' preaching must as such be in some way the effective first stage in the realisation of the Kingdom of God—this thought belongs not alone to *our* ethical sentiment, but it animated also the preaching of Jesus, for he wrought out in strong relief the social character of his ethics. This explains the reluctance one feels to admit that the eschatological idea of the Kingdom of God lay at the basis of Jesus' preaching from beginning to end, since *then* one cannot explain how the new moral community which he formed about himself was in his thought organically connected with the Kingdom which was supernaturally to appear.

One glides here unintentionally into a modern line of thought. The idea of development furnishes what we want, allowing us to conceive of the moral community as an initial stage which by constant growth, extensive and intensive, is ever approaching the final stage. The gradually widening circle represents, however, a modern way of viewing history. It is completely foreign to Jesus. Yet even though he cannot have made use of this explanation of ours, the *fact* that this new community stands in an organic relation with the final stage was for him as certain as for us. But because he expected this final stage as a purely supernatural event the connection was not to be apprehended by human reflection, rather it was a *divine secret,* which he illuminated only by pointing to analogies in the processes of nature.

CHAPTER IV

The Secret of the Kingdom of God

1. *The Parables of the Secret of the Kingdom of God*

We have to do here with the "secret of the Kingdom of God" (Mk. 4:11), which is dealt with in the parables of the sower, of the self-growing seed, of the grain of mustard, and of the leaven. We commonly find in these parables the illustration of a constant and gradual unfolding through which the petty initial stage of a development is connected with the glorious final stage. The seed that is sown already contains the harvest, inasmuch as each seed is devised for the production of plant and fruit. They develop from the seed by natural law. So it is likewise with the development of the Kingdom of God from small and obscure beginnings.

This attractive interpretation of the parables takes from them, however, the character of *secrets,* for the illustration of a steady unfolding through the processes of nature is no secret. Hence it is that we fail to understand what the secret is in these parables. We interpret them according to our scientific knowledge of nature which enables us to unite even such different stages as these by the conception of development.

By reason of the immediateness with which the unschooled spirit of olden time observed the world, nature had, however, still secrets to offer,—in the fact, namely, that she produced two utterly distinct conditions in a sequence, the connection of which was just as certain as it was inexplicable. This immediateness is the note of

Jesus' parables. The conception of development in nature which is contemplated in the modern explanation is not at all brought into prominence, but the exposition is rather devised to place the two conditions so immediately side by side that one is compelled to raise the question, How can the final stage proceed from the initial stage?

1. A man sowed seed. A great part of the seed was lost on account of circumstances the most diverse—and yet the produce of the corn which fell upon good ground was so great that it restored the seed sown thirty, sixty, even an hundred fold.

The detailed interpretation of the description of this loss, and the application to particular classes of men, as it lies before us in Mk. 4:13–20, is the product of a later view which perceived no longer any secret in the parable. Originally, however, the single points of the description were not independent, but the seed which was lost upon the path, or upon the stony ground, or among the thorns, together with that which the fowls of heaven devoured, constituted altogether a unified contrast to that which fell upon good ground. The manner in which it was destroyed has no importance for the parable. In spite of the description so wonderfully wrought out, this saying of Jesus expresses one single thought: So small, considering all that was lost, was the sowing; and yet the harvest so great!—Therein lies the secret.

2. A man scattered seed upon the ground. He slept, went about his affairs, and concerned himself no further about the seed. Before he realised it the harvest stood already in the field, and he could send his servants to gather it in. How did it come to pass that after the seed was sunk in the earth the ground *of itself* brought forth the blade, the ear, and the full corn?—That is the secret.

3. A grain of mustard seed was sown; from it sprouted

a great shrub, with branches under which the birds of the heaven could lodge. How did it come to pass, since the mustard seed is so small?—That is the secret.

4. A woman added a little leaven to a great mass of dough. Afterwards the whole lump was "leaven." How can a little leaven leaven a whole great lump?—That is the secret.

These parables are not at all devised to be interpreted and understood; rather they are calculated to make the hearers observant of the fact that in the affairs of the Kingdom of God a secret is preparing like that which they experience in nature. They are *signals*. As the harvest follows upon the seed-sowing, without it being possible for any one to say how it comes about; so, as the sequel to Jesus' preaching, will the Kingdom of God come with power. Small as is the circle which he gathers about himself in comparison with the greatness of God's Kingdom, it is none the less certain that the Kingdom will come as a consequence of this moral renewal, restricted as it is in scope. It is no less confidently to be expected than that the seed, which while he speaks is slumbering in the ground, will bring forth a glorious harvest. Watch not only for the harvest, but watch for the Kingdom of God! —so speaks the spiritual sower to the Galileans at the season of the seed-sowing. They ought to have the presentiment that the moral renewal in consequence of his preaching stands in a necessary but inexplicable connection with the dawning of the Kingdom of God. The same God who through his mysterious power in nature brings the harvest to pass will also bring to pass the Kingdom of God.

Therefore, when it was the season of the harvest, he sent his Disciples forth to proclaim: The Kingdom of God is at hand.

2. *The Secret of the Kingdom of God in the Address to the People after the Mission of the Twelve*

Jesus was alone. The Disciples carried the news of the nearness of the Kingdom throughout the cities of Israel. While the people thronged him there came the emissaries of the Baptist with their question. He dismissed them with the answer: the Kingdom stands before the door, one needs only the language of the signs and wonders in order to understand. Turning to the people he speaks of the significance of the Baptist and of his office. With this he lets drop a hint of mystery (Mt. 11:14, "If you are able to conceive it," Mt. 11:15, "he that hath ears to hear, let him hear"). John is Elijah, i.e. the personality whose advent marks the immediate dawning of the Kingdom. "From the days of John the Baptist until this moment the Kingdom of Heaven suffereth violence, and men of violence take it by force. For all the Prophets and the Law prophesied until John; and, if ye are able to conceive it, this is Elijah, which is to come. He that hath ears to hear, let him hear" (Mt. 11:12–14).

This saying resists all exegesis, for it does not in the least contain the thought that the individuals gain access to the Kingdom by force. What might that mean anyway? In what sense does that come to pass from the days of the Baptist on? The picture which Jesus employs is unintelligible if it has to do with the entrance of individuals into the Kingdom. It remains just as incomprehensible, however, if it is supposed to refer to the realisation of the Kingdom through gradual development. In the first place, the image of an act of violence contradicts the notion of development; in the second place, the beginning of this compelling force must be dated not from John but from Jesus.

It is a question of the secret of the Kingdom of God,—

hence the hint: He that hath ears to hear, let him hear. This phrase occurs only in connection with the parables of the secret of the Kingdom and as the conclusion of apocalyptic sayings (cf. the use of the expression in the Apocalypse: 2:7, 11, 17, 29; 3:6, 13, 22). Repentance and moral renewal in prospect of the Kingdom of God are like a pressure which is exerted in order to compel its appearance. This movement had begun with the days of the Baptist. The men of violence who take it by force are they which put into practice the moral renewal. They draw it with power down to the earth.

The saying in the speech about the Baptist and the parables of the Kingdom of God mutually explain and supplement one another. The parables bring chiefly into prominence the *incommensurateness* of the relation between the moral renewal that is practised and the consummation of the Kingdom of God, while the image in the speech after the Mission dwells more upon the compelling connection between the two.

3. *The Secret of the Kingdom of God in the Light of the Prophetic and Jewish Expectation*

Jesus' ethics is closely connected with that of the Old Testament prophets, inasmuch as both are alike conditioned by the expectation of a state of perfection which God is to bring about. But also the secret of the Kingdom of God, according to which the moral renewal hastens the supernatural coming of the Kingdom, corresponds with the fundamental thought of the Prophets. In the case of the Prophets, the relation between the moral reform which they would bring about and the glorious condition which God will bring to pass at the Day of Judgment is not that of a mere temporal sequence, but it rests upon a supernatural causal connection. Godless behaviour brings nearer the Day of Judgment and of condemnation. Therefore, God chastises the people and gives them into the hand of their oppressors. When, however, they determine to reform their ways, when they seek refuge in him alone with trusting faith, when righteousness and truth prevail among them, then will the Lord deliver them from their oppressors, and his glory will be manifest over Israel, to whom the heathen will do service. In that day there will then be peace poured out over the whole world, over nature as well as man.

After the Exile this thought was still operative in the conception of the Law. By the observance of the Law the promised glorious estate will be wrung from God. Not the individual but the collectivity influences God through the Law. This generic mode of thought is the primary, the individual mode is secondary. "Israel would be redeemed if only it observed two Sabbaths faithfully."[1] Here we meet with the early prophetic thought in legalistic form.

In general, however, it was the individualistic view which prevailed later. The Law, and moral conduct in general were only the preparation for the expected estate of glory. The lively generic view of the Prophets was replaced by individualistic and lifeless conception. Eschatology became a problem of accounting and ethics became casuistry.

Jesus, however, reached back after the fundamental conception of the prophetic period, and it is only the *form* in which he conceives of the emergence of the final event which bears the stamp of later Judaism. He no longer conceives of it as an intervention of God in the history of the nations, as did the Prophets; but rather as a final cosmical catastrophe. His eschatology is the apocalyptic

[1] Schabbath 118*b*. Wünsche, *System der altsynagogalen Palästinensischen Theologie,* 1880, p. 299.

of the book of Daniel, since the Kingdom is to be brought about by the Son of Man when he appears upon the clouds of heaven (Mk. 8:38; 9:1).

The secret of the Kingdom of God is therefore the synthesis effected by a sovereign spirit between the early prophetic ethics and the apocalyptic of the book of Daniel. Hence it is that Jesus' eschatology was rooted in his age and yet stands so high above it. For his contemporaries it was a question of *waiting for* the Kingdom, of excogitating and depicting every incident of the great catastrophe, and of preparing for the same; while for Jesus it was a question of *bringing to pass* the expected event through the moral renovation. *Eschatological ethics is transformed into ethical eschatology.*

4. *The Secret of the Kingdom of God and the Assumption of a Fortunate Galilean Period*

According to the secret of the Kingdom of God, the coming of the Kingdom is not dependent upon the broad success of Jesus' preaching. Indeed, he expressly emphasises the fact that the limitation of the circle which performs the moral renovation stands in no relation whatever to the all-embracing greatness of the Kingdom which is to come about by reason of their conduct. It suffices that a scanty part of the seed falls upon good ground—and the overplentiful harvest is there, through God's power. Not by the multitude but by the men of violence is the Kingdom compelled to appear.

Hence the secret of the Kingdom of God makes the assumption of a fortunate Galilean period entirely superfluous. Jesus can enjoy the expectation of the speedy realisation of the Kingdom even when he experiences the greatest ill success and when whole districts close themselves against his preaching. They do not thereby delay the coming of the Kingdom of God but only deliver themselves to the judgment, for the Kingdom comes necessarily by reason of the moral renewal of the circle which gathered about Jesus.

The justice of this interpretation of the secret of the Kingdom of God is shown therefore, in the fact that it renders unnecessary, as an explanation of Jesus' life, an assumption which is otherwise absolutely unavoidable but cannot in any way be historically confirmed.

5. *The Secret of the Kingdom of God and the Universalism of Jesus*

So long as the moral renewal upon the basis of Jesus' preaching is brought into relation with the realisation of the Kingdom through the modern thought of evolutionary development the factor correlative to the perfection of the Kingdom is likewise modern, that is, "humanity as a moral whole." One attributes then to Jesus' reflection upon the growth of the new moral community which he founded, foresight of its gradual extension till it embraces the whole of Israel—here, however, the thought of Jesus stops; one may not attribute to him universalistic ideas, for the commission to the Disciples shows that he did not reflect about a moral renewal beyond the borders of Israel. (Mt. 10:5, 6) : Go not into any way of the Gentiles, and enter not into any city of the Samaritans: but go rather to the lost sheep of the house of Israel.

The preaching of the Kingdom of God is therefore particularistic; the Kingdom itself, however, is universalistic, "for they shall come from the east and from the west, from the north and from the south." The generation which required a miracle shall experience such: The Ninevites shall arise at the Day of Judgment and condemn it, because they repented at the preaching of Jonah, "and here is a greater than Jonah." Also the Queen of the South shall rise in judgment against the contemporaries of Jesus, because she came from the ends of the earth to hear the wisdom of Solomon, "and behold, a greater than Solomon is here" (Mt. 12:41, 42).

For the modern consciousness, because it applies to everything the rubrics of evolution, there is an insuperable contradiction between the particularism of the preaching of the Kingdom and the universalism of its consummation. In the secret of the Kingdom of God, however, particularism and universalism go together. The Kingdom is universalistic, for it arises out of a cosmic act by which God awakes unto glory the righteous of all times and of all peoples. The bringing about of the Kingdom, on the other hand, is dependent upon particularism, for it is to be forced to approach by the moral renewal of the contemporaries of Jesus. Salvation comes out of Israel.

6. *The Secret of the Kingdom of God and Jesus' Attitude towards the Law and the State*

Jesus did not declare himself either for the Law or against it. He recognised it simply as an existing fact without binding himself to it. He felt no obligation to decide in principle whether it was to be regarded as binding or as not binding. For him this was a question of no practical importance. The real concern was the new morality, not the Law. This Law was for him holy and inviolable in so far as it pointed the way to the new morality. But therewith it did away with itself, for in the Kingdom which comes into being an account of the new morality the Law is abrogated, since the accomplished condition is super-legal and super-ethical. Up to this point it had a right to last. Whether the Law should also be binding upon his followers in the future was a question which did not exist for Jesus; it was history which first proposed this problem to the primitive Church.

It was the same with regard to the State. The question which was put to him in the Jerusalem days had for him no practical importance. As he replied to the Pharisees' question, whether one should give tribute to Cæsar, he had no thought of defining his attitude towards the State or determining that of his followers. How could any one be concerned at all about such things! The State was simply earthly, therefore ungodly, domination. Its duration extended, therefore, only to the dawn of God's dominion. As this was near at hand, what need had one to decide if one would be tributary to the world-power or no? One might as well submit to it, its end was in fact near. Give to Cæsar what is Cæsar's and to God what is God's (Mk. 12:17)—this word is uttered with a sovereign irony against the Pharisees, who understood so little the signs of the time that this still appeared to them a question of importance. They are just as foolish in the matter of the Kingdom of God as the Sadducees with their catch-question to which husband the seven times married wife should belong at the resurrection; for they, too, leave one thing out of account—the power of God (Mk. 12:24).

7. *The Modern Element in Jesus' Eschatology*

"Let it be the maxim in every scientific investigation for one to pursue undisturbed the due course of it with all possible exactitude and frankness, not considering what it may collide with outside of its own field, but following it out, so far as one can, truly and completely for itself alone. Frequent observation has convinced me that when one has brought this task to an end, that which in the midst of it appeared to me for the time being very questionable with respect to other teaching outside, if only I closed my eyes to this questionableness and attended merely to my task till it was finished, finally in unexpected wise proved to be in perfect agreement with those very teachings,—though the truth had presented itself without the least reference to those teachings, without partiality and prejudice for them." [2]

Kant uttered this profound word at the moment when the correspondence of the notion of transcendental freedom with the practical first occurred to him. The case is the same with the relation of Jesus' ethics to his eschatology. It is a postulate of our Christian conviction that the ethics of Jesus in its basic thoughts is modern. Hence we come back again and again to the search after the modern element in his ethics, and for this cause we force into the background his eschatology, since it appears to us unmodern. If, however, one resolves to ignore for a moment this interest, which is so deeply grounded in our being and so well justified, and regards the relation of Jesus' eschatology to his ethics simply for itself, as a purely historical question, the investigation brings to light the astonishing result that the latter (i.e. Jesus' ethics) is modern in a far higher degree than any one hitherto has dared to hope. Jesus' ethics is modern, not because the eschatology can be reduced somehow to a mere accompaniment, but precisely because the ethics is absolutely dependent upon this eschatology! The fact is, this eschatology itself, as it is exhibited in the secret of the Kingdom of God, is thoroughly modern, inasmuch as it is dominated by the thought that the Kingdom of God is to come by reason of the religious-moral renovation which the believers perform. *Every moral-religious performance is therefore labour for the coming of the Kingdom of God.*

[2] *Kritik der praktischen Vernunft.* Ed. Reclam, p. 129.

As the eschatology in this ethical-eschatological *Weltanschauung* gradually faded in the course of history, there remained an ethical *Weltanschauung* in which the eschatology persisted in the form of an imperishable faith in the final triumph of the good. The secret of the Kingdom of God contains the secret of the whole Christian *Weltanschauung*. The ethical eschatology of Jesus is the *heroic form* in which the modern-Christian *Weltanschauung* first entered into history!

CHAPTER V

The Secret of the Kingdom of God in the Thought of the Passion

In the last period of his life Jesus again uttered parables of the Kingdom of God: God's vineyard (Mt. 21:33–46); the royal marriage (Mt. 22:1–14); the servant watching (Mt. 24:42–47); the ten virgins (Mt. 25:1–13); the talents (Mt. 25:14–30).

These parables, in contrast to those about the secret of the Kingdom, contain no secret, but rather they are teaching parables pure and simple, from which a moral is to be drawn. The Kingdom of God is near. Those only will be found to belong to it who by their moral conduct are prepared for it.

The second period contains instead the *secret of the Passion.* Jesus' utterances, as we have seen, point to a mysterious causal connection between the Passion and the coming of the Kingdom, because the eschatology and the thought of the Passion always emerge side by side, and the Disciples' expectation of the future is in every case roused to the highest pitch by the proclamation of his suffering.

The secret of the Passion takes up, therefore, the secret of the Kingdom of God and carries it further. To the moral renewal which, according to the secret of the Kingdom of God, exercises a compelling power upon the coming of the Kingdom, there is adjoined another factor—*the redeeming death of Jesus.* That completes the penitence of those who believe in the coming of the Kingdom. Therewith Jesus comes to the aid of the men of violence who are compelling the approach of the Kingdom. The power which he thereby exerts is the highest conceivable—he gives up his life.

The idea of the Passion is therefore the transformation of the secret of the Kingdom of God. Hence it is no more designed to be understood than are the parables of the secret of the Kingdom. In each case it is a question of a fact which can be probed no further.

The connection between the thought of the Passion and the secret of the Kingdom of God guarantees the continuity of Jesus' world of thought. All constructions which have been devised with a view to establishing this continuity have proved insufficient to accomplish what was expected of them. The acceptance of the thought of the Passion means in all cases a complete change in his idea of the Kingdom and in his *Weltanschauung*. If, however, one places the thought of the Passion in the great context of the secret of the Kingdom of God, the continuity is furnished naturally. The thought of the supernatural introduction of the Kingdom of God runs through the whole of Jesus' life: the idea of the Passion is merely the fashion in which it is formulated in the second period.

How comes it that the secret of the Kingdom of God takes the form of the secret of the Passion?

Why must the atonement of Jesus be added to complete the moral renewal and the penitence of the community which believes in the Kingdom?

In what sense has the redeeming death of Jesus an influence upon the coming of the Kingdom?

CHAPTER VI

The Character Ascribed to Jesus on the Ground of His Public Ministry

1. *The Problem and the Facts*

The experience at the Baptism signified the inception of Jesus' messianic consciousness. In the neighbourhood of Cæsarea Philippi he revealed his secret to the Disciples. It was before the High Priest that he first openly made profession of his messianic office. Therefore the messianic consciousness underlay all the while his preaching of the Kingdom of God. But he does not assume on the part of his hearers any knowledge of the position which belonged to him. The faith which he required had nothing to do with his person, but it was due only to the message of the nearness of the Kingdom. It was the Fourth Evangelist who first presented the history of Jesus as if it concerned itself chiefly with his personality.

We cannot estimate how far his real character may have shone through his message, for such as had an awakened understanding. One thing is certain: up to the time of the mission of the Twelve no one had the faintest idea of recognising in him the Messiah. At Cæsarea Philippi the Disciples could only reply that the people took him for a prophet or for Elijah the Forerunner, and they themselves knew no better, for Peter, as Jesus himself said, did not derive his knowledge from the Master's ministry in work and word, but owed it to a supernatural revelation.

The Synoptical notices must be judged in accordance with this fundamental fact. In the first place, there is a series of Matthean passages which stand at variance with it.

Mt. 9:27–31: In the Galilean parallel to the healing of the blind man at Jericho it is related that two blind men pursued him through the whole village with the cry, "Son of David." What Jesus means by the warning, "See that no man knows it," remains indeed obscure.

Mt. 12:23: After a miraculous healing the people whisper to themselves whether this is not the Son of David.

Mt. 14:33: After their experience at sea in the boat the Disciples fall down before him saying, "Truly thou art the Son of God."

Mt. 15:22: The Canaanitish woman addresses him as the Son of David,—whereas according to Mark she simply falls at his feet and cries for help.

All of these passages are peculiar to Matthew and belong to a secondary literary stratum. For the history of Jesus they have no importance, but a great deal for the history of the history of Jesus. They show us, that is, how the later time was inclined even more and more to depict his life in harmony with the presumption that he not only knew himself to be the Messiah but that others also had this impression of him.

In the second place, it is a question of the speeches of the demoniacs. According to Mk. 3:11 the unclean spirits, as often as they saw him, threw themselves at his feet and addressed him as the Son of God (cf. also Mk. 1:24, 57). It is true, he rebuked this cry and commanded silence. But if we did not have the incontestably sure information that during the whole of his Galilean ministry the people knew no more than that he was a prophet or Elijah, we should be forced to assume that these cries of the demoniacs made the people somehow aware of his true character. As it is, however, we may discern with precision, from the fact that the demon-cries were ignored, how very far men were from suspecting him to be the Messiah. Who believed the devil and the wild speech of the possessed?

In the third place, it is a question of the expression "Son of Man." If Jesus used it as a self-designation before Cæsarea Philippi, that would constitute in each case a messianic suggestion, for every one must refer this expression of the book of Daniel to the person who was to characterise the last time.

According to Mark, Jesus twice employed this expression as a self-designation *before* Cæsarea Philippi (Mk. 2:10; 2:28), and it occurs in the same sense in a series of passages peculiar to Matthew (Mt. 8:20; 11:19; 12:32, 40; 13:37, 41 and 16:13). In judging these passages also one must proceed from the sure ground which is furnished by the reply of the Disciples at Cæsarea Philippi.

Either Jesus had not used this expression up to that time, in which case these Son of Man passages are chronologically anticipated, and constitute a mere literary phenomena.

Or else he had used the expression. Then he must have done so in such a way that no man could suppose that he assumed for himself the dignity of the Son of Man of Daniel.

The problem in the second period is still harder. The Disciples knew his secret, but they dared reveal it to no one. But how about the people? Did they now have a presentiment of the messianic dignity of Jesus?

The problem has to do therefore with three facts:

1. The whole discussion in the Jerusalem days turns in no wise upon the messianic dignity of Jesus, but has

to do rather with legal propositions and with questions of the day. Far too little weight has been attached hitherto to the fact that neither the people nor the scribes took up a position towards him as the messianic personality. How different the Jerusalem days would have been if the question which agitated them was: Is he the Messiah—is he not? can he be—can he not? In reality he is merely the unofficial authority of the Galilean people, before whom the scholars of the capital bring their questions of the school, whether with a sincere mind, or with the perfidious intention of destroying his authority.

2. In the second period Jesus had the people about him only for a few days,—from the crossing of the Jordan until his death. During this time he made to them no disclosure about his messiahship, and gave them also no hint which they could and must understand in this sense. The bribed witnesses know nothing of the sort to allege. What is remarkable in their evidence—upon which too little weight has been laid—consists precisely in the fact that *they in no wise charge him with wishing to be the Messiah.* For them his impious pretension exhausts itself in a disrespectful word about the Temple. Let one picture to himself what the procedure of the trial would have been if the hired accusers had of themselves discovered messianic hints in Jesus' speeches!

3. From this point one arrives necessarily at the conclusion that up to the last moment he was for the people in Jerusalem just what he was in Galilee,—the great Prophet or the Forerunner, but in no wise the Messiah! There are two facts, however, which do not comport with this.

The entrance into Jerusalem was—according to the common apprehension—*a messianic ovation.* Therefore the people must have had a presentiment of Jesus' dignity.

The High Priest put to him the question, whether he were the Messiah. Therefore he knew of Jesus' claim.

We have here a clear question to deal with: was Jesus regarded in the Jerusalem days as a messianic pretendant or no? One should not obscure this question by speaking of a more or less clear "presentiment" in this matter. The "presentiment of the messiahship of Jesus" is a modern invention. The populace would hardly be swayed hither and yon by a dark mysterious presentiment, but rather it must have been a question of belief or unbelief. Whosoever held that he was the Messiah must accompany him through fire and death—to glory. Whosoever held no such faith, but had only a presentiment of such a pretension on his part, must give the signal to stone the blasphemer. There was no third course.

The facts in general speak in favour of the opinion that the people and the Pharisees in the Jerusalem days ascribed to Jesus no messianic pretension,—no more indeed than they did at an earlier period. Only in this case the entrance into Jerusalem, understood as a messianic ovation, remains an enigma, and it is likewise unaccountable how it occurred to the High Priest to question him about his messiahship.

On the one hand the situation must be understood in the way which is commonly assumed. Then one must renounce every hope of an historical understanding of the last public period of Jesus. It will not do to suppose that at the beginning of this period (entrance into Jerusalem) and at the end of it (question of the High Priest at the trial) he was taken for the Messiah, while the Jerusalem days which lay in the interval knew nothing of this claim whatever.

Or else—the entrance into Jerusalem and the question of the High Priest have not been rightly and historically understood. Was the ovation offered to the messianic pretendant? Did the High Priest in his question give utterance to something which all knew? Did he deduce the claim of messiahship from Jesus' life, activity, and speech? —or did he perhaps learn through betrayal the innermost secret of Jesus, which since Cæsarea Philippi was known only to his trusted intimates?

The problem of Jesus' messiahship in all its difficulty may be formulated as follows: How was it possible that Jesus knew himself as the Messiah from the beginning, and yet to the very last moment did not give in his public preaching any intimation of his messiahship? How could it in the long run remain hidden from the people that these speeches were uttered out of a messianic consciousness? *Jesus was a Messiah who during his public ministry would not be one, did not need to be, and might not be, for the sake of fulfilling his mission! It is thus that history puts the problem.*

2. *Jesus Is Elijah through His Solidarity with the Son of Man*

What character could and must the people ascribe to Jesus on the ground of his public ministry? That is the question with which we have now to do.

The Messiah and the messianic Kingdom belong inseparably together. Hence if Jesus had preached a present messianic Kingdom, it would have been at the same time incumbent upon him to indicate the Messiah,—he would have had to begin by legitimating himself as the Messiah before the people.

The fact is, however, that he preached a future kingdom. With this the possibility was completely excluded that any one could suppose him to be the Messiah. *If the Kingdom was future, so also was the Messiah.* If Jesus nevertheless had messianic pretensions, this thought was thoroughly remote from the people, for his preaching of the Kingdom excluded even the least conjecture of the sort. Hence even the cries of the demons did not avail to put the people on the right track.

Conjectures of that sort were rendered completely impossible by the way in which Jesus spoke of the Messiah in the third person and as a character of the future. He intimated to the Disciples as he sent them upon their mission that the Son of Man would appear before they had gone through all the cities of Israel (Mt. 10:23). In Mk. 8:38 he gave promise to the people of the speedy appearing of the Son of Man for judgment and the coming of the Kingdom of God with power. In the same way at Jerusalem he still spoke of the judgment which the Son of Man will hold when he appears in his glory surrounded by the angels (Mt. 25:31).

Only the Disciples after the revelation of Cæsarea Philippi, and the High Priest after the "Yes" of Jesus, could trace a personal relation between him and the Son of Man of whose coming he spoke,—for they knew his secret. For his other hearers, however, *Jesus of Nazareth* and the individual who was the subject of his discourse, the *Son of Man,* remained two entirely distinct personalities.

Before the people Jesus merely suggested the *absolute solidarity* between himself and the Son of Man whom he proclaimed.

It was only in this form that his own gigantic personality obtruded in his preaching of the Kingdom of God. Only he who under all conditions confesses him, the proclaimer of the coming of the Son of Man, will be discovered as a member of the Kingdom at the Day of Judgment. Jesus, in fact, will intervene before God and before the Son of Man in his behalf (Mk. 8:38; 9:1; Mt. 10:32, 33). One must be ready to give up the dearest things to follow him, for only so can one show one's self *worthy of him* (Mt. 10:37, 38). Hence Jesus is grieved when the rich young man cannot make up his mind to give up his riches in order to follow him (Mk. 10:22), for now he cannot appear for him at the Day of Judgment to insure that he shall be accepted as a member of the Kingdom of God. Still, in the measureless omnipotence of God he finds reason to hope that this rich man will nevertheless find entrance into the Kingdom (Mk. 10:17–31). If this man, therefore, because Jesus cannot intervene in his behalf, is not sure "to inherit eternal life" (Mk. 10:17), those, on the other hand who, confessing him and his message, endure death are certain to save their life, *i.e.* to be found as members of the Kingdom at the resurrection of the dead (Mk. 8:37). Hence in the beginning of the sermon on the mount he pronounces them blessed who for his sake suffer reviling and persecution, because thereby, like the meek and the merciful, they are designated as members of the Kingdom (Mt. 5:11, 12).

From Jesus' standpoint, this absolute solidarity between God and the Son of Man on the one hand, and himself on the other presented no enigma, for it was based upon his messianic self-consciousness; he can speak thus because he is conscious of being himself the Son of Man. It was quite different for the people, and for the Disciples before the revelation at Cæsarea Philippi. How can Jesus of Nazareth, in a manner so sovereignly self-confident, proclaim his absolute solidarity with the Son of Man? This assertion forced the people to reflect upon his personality. Who was this whose manifestation mightily extended out of the premessianic and into the messianic æon itself, so that God and the Son of Man receive into the Kingdom such as had confessed him, if this confession did not lose its value by reason of the defect of moral worthiness, as he himself once expressly declared by way of warning? Such importance as Jesus claimed for himself belonged to only *one* personality,—Elijah, the mighty Forerunner,—for his manifestation stretched out of the present into the messianic æon and bound both together. Hence the people held that Jesus was Elijah. In this was expressed the highest estimate which Jesus' personality could wring from the masses. In this case it is not a question of one of the customary misunderstandings so beloved of the secondary Gospel narrators, but the people *could not,* from Jesus' appearance and proclamation, come to any other conclusion about him.

3. *Jesus Is Elijah through the Signs which Proceed from Him*

In order to render intelligible the attitude of Jesus' contemporaries towards himself and his work, we must rid ourselves of two false presuppositions with which we constantly though unconsciously operate. First, the expectation at that time was not fixed upon the Messiah but upon the Forerunner promised by prophecy. Secondly, no one in any way detected this Forerunner in the person of the Baptist. Both of our presuppositions run precisely to the contrary effect, and thereby we spoil our historical perspective.

The appearing of the Messiah in conjunction with the great crisis which he brings about constitutes the supernatural drama which the world awaits. But before the curtain rises there must arise among the expectant sons of men the man who is to speak the prologue of the piece; who then, so soon as the curtain is lifted, associates himself with the celestial personages which conduct the action of the drama. Hence men are in expectancy first of all not for the rising of the curtain and the appearing of the Messiah but for the speaker of the prologue. *It was important to signalise the entrance of the Forerunner upon the stage in order to know to what hour the hand of the world clock pointed.*

Elijah, however, had not as yet appeared, for the Baptist had not legitimated himself as such. He lacked to this end the display of supernatural power. Signs and wonders, however, belonged necessarily to the epoch which immediately preceded the Kingdom. A general pouring out of the Spirit and prophesying, wonders in heaven and upon earth,—all that was to occur before the Day of God comes. So it was defined by the prophet Joel (3:28 ff). Peter in his sermon at Pentecost appealed to this passage (Acts 2:17–22). One ought to recognise from the supernatural ecstatic "tongues" that one is approaching the end of the days. The crucified Jesus hath God raised up to to be the Messiah in the Resurrection, and the Kingdom will soon dawn.

This passage in Joel was therefore applied to the time immediately preceding the messianic age, the time of miracles, in which according to the prophecy of Malachi the Forerunner should appear (Mal. 3:23, 24). Moreover, the selfsame refrain unites these two fundamental passages of premessianic expectation: Mal. 4:5 is the same as Joel 2:37—"Before the coming of the great and terrible Day of the Lord." *The Forerunner without miracles in an unmiraculous age was therefore unthinkable.*

For the contemporaries the characteristic difference between John and Jesus consisted precisely in the fact that the one simply pointed to the nearness of the Kingdom of God while the other confirmed his preaching by signs and wonders. Men had the consciousness of entering with

Jesus upon the age of miracles. He was the Baptist,—but the Baptist, as it were, translated into the supernatural. After the mission of the Twelve, as his emergence and his signs became known abroad together with the news of the death of the Baptist, people said: The Baptist is raised from the dead. Hence the Disciples answered him at Cæsarea Philippi that men took him for Elijah or for the Baptist (Mk. 8:28). Herod as he heard of him would not give up the notion that he was the Baptist: "The Baptist is risen from the dead, and therefore do these powers work in him" (Mk. 6:14).

Also the significance which Jesus ascribed to the signs must have led his hearers to suppose that they were in the midst of the era of the Forerunner. Their significance consisted, namely, in the fact that they confirmed the nearness of the messianic Kingdom. The people ought to believe him for the sake of the signs and repent unto the Kingdom of God.

The signs are an act of God's grace through which he would make men aware what hour it is. Whosoever does not repent is damned. So it comes to pass with the inhabitants of Chorazin, Bethsaida, and Capernaum. But whosoever blasphemes against the Holy Ghost and ascribes the signs to the power of ungodliness has no forgiveness in eternity. The scribes from Jerusalem made themselves guilty in Galilee of this offence (Mk. 3:22 ff). Those, however, who did not harden themselves held that the Kingdom of God stands at the door and that Jesus is the Forerunner, because they had evidently entered the age of signs which the Scripture had prophesied.

4. *The Victory over Demons and the Secret of the Kingdom of God*

For Jesus the signs signified the nearness of the Kingdom in a sense still higher than the purely temporal, chronological nearness. By his victory over the demons he was conscious of *influencing the coming of it.* The secret of the Kingdom of God plays into this conception. The thought is contained in the parable with which he repels the false suspicions of the Jerusalem scribes (Mk. 3:23, 30).

The meaning of this parable is, in fact, not exhausted by the thought that evil spirits do not undermine their own dominion by rising up one against another. In the concluding word we encounter unexpectedly the "now and then" which is characteristic of the secret of the Kingdom of God: "No one can enter into the house of the strong man and spoil his goods, except he *first* bind the strong man, and *then* he will spoil his house." The casting out of demons, therefore, signified for Jesus the binding of the power of ungodliness and rendering it harmless. Hence this activity, like the moral renewal in the secret of the Kingdom, stands in causal relation with the dawning of the Kingdom of God. Through his conquest of the demons Jesus is the man of violence who compels the approach of the Kingdom. For when the power of ungodliness is bound, then comes the moment when the dominion shall be taken from it. In order that this may happen it must first be rendered harmless. Hence in sending the Disciples upon their mission Jesus not only commands them to proclaim the nearness of the Kingdom, but he also gives them authority over the demons (Mt. 10:1). In that moment of highest eschatological expectation he sends them out as the men of violence who are to deal the last blow. The repentance which is to be accomplished by their preaching, and the overcoming of the power of ungodliness in the demoniacs, work together for the hastening of the Kingdom.

Thus the parables of the secret of the Kingdom (Mk. 4), the parable in Jesus' apology to the Pharisees (Mk. 3:23, 30), and the parable in the eulogy of the Baptist (Mt. 11:12, 15) all express the same thought. The two latter correspond even in the drastic image of violent action, when the notion of "robbery" is common to them both (Mk. 3:27; Mt. 11:12).

For Jesus' consciousness the healing of the demoniacs was therefore a part of the secret of the Kingdom of God. It sufficed for the people, however, to grasp the purely chronological connection.

5. *Jesus and the Baptist*

We have seen above that no one could recognise Elijah in the person of the Baptist because his ministry and preaching without miracle did not correspond with the Scriptural representation of the Forerunner's time. None thought of ascribing to him this office and dignity except —for there was one exception—*Jesus*! He it was that first gave the people a mysterious hint that this man was the Forerunner: "If ye are willing to receive it, he himself is Elijah, the coming-one" (Mt. 11:14). He is aware, however, that with this he is giving utterance to an incomprehensible secret which to his hearers remains just as obscure as the word uttered in the same connection about the men of violence who since the days of the Baptist compel the Kingdom (Mt. 11:12). Hence he concludes both these sayings with the oracular phrase: He that hath ears to hear, let him hear (Mt. 11:15).

The people, however, were very far from comprehending that this Baptist who had fallen into the hands of Herod could be the prodigious personality who was to stand upon the threshold between the premessianic and the messianic age. So the mysterious word of Jesus died upon the air, and the people stuck to the opinion that John was really a prophet (Mk. 11:32).

The rulers also could reach no conclusion about the personality of the Baptist. For this reason they were worsted in their colloquy with Jesus when they would challenge him for his purifying of the Temple (Mk. 11:33).

The case was quite the same with the Disciples: they were incapable by themselves of recognising in John the expected Elijah. On the descent from the Mount of Transfiguration they were assailed by scruples about the messiahship of Jesus and about the possibility of the resurrection of the dead which Jesus had touched upon in his discourse. This assumed, indeed, that the messianic era was already present, and this could not yet have dawned, for "Elijah must first come, as the scribes demonstrate" (Mk. 9:9–11). Thereupon Jesus replied to them that John was this Elijah, even though he was delivered into the power of men (Mk. 9:12, 13).

How did Jesus arrive at the conviction that the Baptist was Elijah? It was through a necessary inference from his own messiahship. Because he knew himself to be the Messiah, the other must be Elijah. Between the two ideas there was a necessary correspondence. No one could know that the Baptist was Elijah except he derived this cognisance from the messiahship of Jesus. No one could arrive at the thought that John was Elijah without at the same time being obliged to see in Jesus the Messiah. For after the Forerunner there remained no place for a second manifestation of the kind. No one knew that Jesus took himself to be the Messiah. Therefore in the Baptist men perceived a prophet and raised the question whether Jesus were not Elijah. No one understood in their full bearing the mysterious concluding sentences of the eulogy over the Baptist. *Only for Jesus was John the promised Elijah.*

6. *The Baptist and Jesus*

What was the Baptist's attitude to Jesus? If he had been conscious of being the Forerunner, he must have surmised that Jesus was the Messiah. One generally assumes this and supposes that he as the Forerunner put the question to Jesus whether he were the Messiah (Mt. 11:2–6). This supposition seems to us perfectly natural because we always represent to ourselves the two characters in the relation of Forerunner-Messiah.

In this connection, however, we forget a perfectly obvious question. Did the Baptist feel himself to be Elijah, the Forerunner? In no utterance before the people did he raise such a claim. They stubbornly recognised in him only a prophet. Also during his imprisonment he can have claimed no such thing, for in Jerusalem the people still held to the same opinion, that he was a prophet.

If somehow or another the presentiment had prevailed that he represented the character of Elijah, how then could men generally get the notion that John was a prophet, Jesus the Elijah? That this was the general view even after the death of the Baptist, is proved by the reply of the Disciples at Cæsarea Philippi.

To view the Baptist's query under the presumption that the Forerunner is asking whether Jesus be the Messiah is to put the question in a light which is completely unjustified; for whether John took himself to be the Forerunner is not in the least to be proven. Therefore it is also by no means made out that his question referred to the messianic dignity. The people standing by, as they did not take John to be the Forerunner, must have interpreted it in a very different way,—namely, in the sense: Art thou Elias?

The fact is that the usual perspective hides a characteristic detail in this very section, the fact, namely, that Jesus applies again to the Baptist the same designation which the Baptist in his question had applied to him! Art thou the Coming One? asked the Baptist. Jesus replied: If ye are willing to receive it, *he himself* is Elijah, the Coming One! The designation of the "Coming One" is therefore common to both speeches, only that we arbitrarily refer it to the Messiah in the question of the Baptist. This proceeding, which appears so natural in the naïve perspective, will show itself to be unjustified so soon as one becomes aware that it is in fact only a question of perspective and not of any real standard. For then the phrase "He himself" in Jesus' reply acquires suddenly an unsuspected significance: "*he himself* is Elijah," the Coming One! This reference compels us to understand by the Coming One in the Baptist's question, not the Messiah, but—as in Jesus' reply—Elias.

"Art thou the expected Forerunner?"—thus the Baptist through his disciples makes inquiry of Jesus. "If ye are able to receive it, he himself is this Forerunner," said Jesus to the people after he had spoken to them about the greatness of the Baptist.

By this reference the scene now receives a far more intense colouring. First of all, it becomes clear why Jesus speaks about the Baptist *after the departure of the messengers.* He feels himself obliged to lead the people up climactically from the conception that John is a prophet to the presentiment that he is the Forerunner, with whose appearing the hand of the world clock nears the fateful hour to which refers the word concerning "him who prepares the way," and of whom the scribes say "that he must first come" (Mk. 9:11).

John, in fact, with his question was backward in his reckoning of the Messianic time. His messengers seek information about the Forerunner at the moment when Jesus' confidence that the Kingdom is immediately to dawn was at the highest pitch. He had just sent out his Disciples and given them to expect that the appearing of the Son of Man might surprise them on their way through the cities of Israel. The hour is already far more advanced—that is what Jesus would give the people to understand in his "eulogy over the Baptist," if they can receive it.

John reached this surmise about Jesus in the same way as did the people. That is to say, as he heard *of the signs and deeds of Jesus* (Mt. 11:2), there occurred to him the thought that this might be something more than a prophet with a call to repentance. So he sends messengers to him in order to have assurance upon this point.

Herewith, however, the proclamation of the Baptist is put in an entirely different light. He never pointed to the coming Messiah, *but to the expected Forerunner.* So is to be explained the proclamation about "him that is to come after him" (Mk. 1:7, 8). As applied to the Messiah, the expressions he uses remain obscure. They denote, that is, only a difference of degree, not a total difference in kind, between himself and the person whom he announces. If he were speaking of the Messiah, it would have been impossible for him to employ these expressions, in which, in spite of the mighty difference in rank, he still compares the Coming One to himself. He thinks of the Forerunner as like himself, baptising and preaching repentance unto the Kingdom, only that he is incomparably greater and mightier. Instead of baptising with water, he will baptise with the Holy Ghost (Mk. 1:8).

This cannot apply to the Messiah. Since when does the Messiah baptise? Then, too, the famous pouring out of the Spirit does not occur within but *before* the messianic era! Before the coming of the great Day of the Lord he will pour out his Spirit upon all flesh, and signs and wonders shall be showed in heaven and on earth (Joel

2:28 ff). Before the coming of the great Day of the Lord he will send Elijah the Prophet (Mal. 4:5). The Baptist combines these two chief indications of the character of the great events that are to precede the Last Time, and he arrives at the conception of the Forerunner who is to baptise with the Holy Ghost! One sees from this what a supernatural light surrounded the figure of the Forerunner in the current conception. Hence it is that John felt himself so little before him.

Jesus was put by this question in a difficult position. The Baptist in asking him, Art thou the Forerunner? or art thou not? had proposed a false alternative to which Jesus could answer neither yes nor no. He was not willing to entrust the secret of his messiahship to the messengers. He therefore replied with a hint of the nearness of the the Kingdom which was revealed in his deeds. At the same time he thrust his own personality mightily into the foreground. He alone can be blessed who stands by him and who finds no occasion of stumbling in him. With this he would say the same as he said once also to the people: membership in the Kingdom is dependent upon one's attachment to him (Mk. 8:38).

Jesus' remarkable, evasive answer to the Baptist, in which exegesis has always believed that it must discover a special finesse, is explained therefore simply by the necessity of the situation. Jesus could not answer directly. Hence he gave this obscure response. The Baptist was to gather from it what he would and could. Besides, it was of no importance how he understood it. Events would soon teach him, for the time is already much further advanced than he supposes, and the hammer is already lifted to strike the hour.

It is exceedingly difficult for us to get rid of the notion that the Baptist and Jesus stood to one another in the relation of Forerunner and Messiah. It is only through intense reflection that we can reach the perception that the two characters stand in this relation in our perspective only because we assume the messiahship of Jesus; but that in order to discover the historical relationship we must calculate and apply the right perspective.

So long as one is still prejudiced in any way by the old perspective, one cannot do justice to the foregoing investigation. That is, one will still have the notion that it is a question of "the forerunner of the Forerunner" and the Forerunner—an ingenious multiplication of the Forerunner by himself. That is falsely expressed. A prophet of repentance, John the Baptist, directs men's attention to the prediction of the mighty figure of Elijah the Forerunner, and as he hears in prison of the signs of Jesus he wonders if this may not be Elijah—and does not dream that this man holds himself to be the Messiah, and that for this reason he himself will henceforth be designated in history as the Forerunner. That is the historical situation.

The moment the conception of history was defined by the conviction that Jesus was the Messiah the historical perspective was necessarily shifted. The Gospels display this shifting in increasing measure. In the introductory verses of Mark the quotation from Malachi about the Forerunner who is to prepare the way (Mal. 3:1) is already applied to John. According to Matthew, the Baptist hears in prison of "the works of the Messiah" (Mt. 11:2). If here it is only a question of the casual and unreflecting introduction of a new mode of conception, the Fourth Gospel, on the other hand, has made a principle of it and consistently represents the history in line with the presumption that because Jesus was the Messiah the Baptist was the Forerunner and must have felt himself to be such. The historical Baptist says: I am not the *Forerunner,* for he is incomparably greater and mightier than I. According to the Fourth Gospel the people could conjecture that he was the Christ. He was obliged to say, therefore: I am not the *Christ* (John 1:20)!

Thus has the relation been altered under the influence of the new perspective. The person of the Baptist has become historically unrecognisable. Finally they have made out of him the modern doubter, who half believed in Jesus' messiahship, and half disbelieved. In this apprehensive indecision, this backing and filling, is supposed to lie, in fact, the tragedy of his existence! Now, however, one may confidently strike him from the list of those characters, so interesting to us moderns, who come to ruin through a tragic half-faith. Jesus spared him that. For so long as he lived he required of no man faith in him as the Messiah—and yet that is what he was!

7. *The Blind Man at Jericho and the Ovation at the Entrance to Jerusalem*

Was the entrance into Jerusalem a messianic ovation? That depends, in the first place, upon how one interprets the cry of the people; but then also, upon one's notion of the encounter between Jesus and the blind man. If it was actually a question there of his being greeted as the Son of David,—a greeting which he no longer repudiates, but tacitly admits, so that the people learn to apprehend what he takes himself to be,—the consequence is inevitable that it was a messianic ovation.

For the exact understanding of the description of Jesus' entrance into Jerusalem, the differences in detail between Mark and the parallels are of far reaching importance. In Mark we have two clearly distinguishable acclamations. The first is directed to the person of Jesus in their midst: "Hosanna! Blessed be 'the Coming One' in the name of the Lord" (Mk. 11:9). The second refers to the expected coming of the Kingdom: "Blessed be the coming Kingdom of our father David. Hosanna in the highest!" The Son of David is thus not mentioned at all!

It is different in Matthew. There the people shout: "Hosanna to the Son of David! Blessed be the Coming One in the name of the Lord. Hosanna in the highest!" (Mt. 21:9). We have here therefore only the cry which was directed to the person of Jesus; the Kingdom is not mentioned; men acclaim instead the Son of David and, at the same time, the Coming One.

Luke's version does not come into account, for he deals with reminiscences from the history of the infancy: "Blessed be the king that cometh in the name of the Lord. Peace in heaven and glory in the highest" (Lk. 19:38).

Thus Matthew in his account interprets the Coming One as the Son of David. We possess no direct proof that this expression (the Coming One), which is derived from Psalm 118:25 ff, was employed in Jesus' time for the Messiah. It has been shown, however, that *the Baptist as well as Jesus applied it rather to the Forerunner Elijah.* It is therefore unhistorical when Matthew represents the people as acclaiming in the same breath both the Coming One and the Son of David.

Mark has here, too, preserved in his detail the original situation. The people acclaimed Jesus as the "Coming One," i.e. as the Forerunner, and sings an "Hosanna in the highest" to the Kingdom which is soon to descend upon earth. A fine distinction is made in the use of *Hosanna* and *Hosanna in the highest* ("places" is to be supplied). The former applies to the Forerunner present in their midst; the latter, to the heavenly Kingdom. The secondary character of the account in Matthew is evident in the fact that it applies to the Son of David and to the Coming One not only an Hosanna but likewise an Hosanna in the highest,—whereby the Messiah is first assumed to be on earth and then, still in heaven! Here it becomes plain that the second Hosanna belonged originally with the Kingdom.

The entrance into Jerusalem, therefore, was an ovation not to the Messiah but to the Forerunner. But then it is impossible that the people understood the scene with the blind man as indicating that Jesus welcomed the address "Son of David."

Here again it is a question of Synoptical detail by which the scene is totally changed. The shout in the name of the Son of David is incidental. The question is only whether the public could and must conceive it as a form of address. This conception is evidently that of Matthew and Luke, *but by Mark it is excluded.*

According to the Matthean account, two blind men sit by the wayside and cry, Have mercy upon us, Son of David (Mt. 20:30).

In Luke the cry runs: Jesus, thou Son of David, have mercy upon me (Lk. 18:38). Thereupon Jesus comes to a stand before him, converses with him, and heals him.

According to Mark, the blind beggar, son of Timæus, is sitting behind the multitude at the edge of the road. *Jesus does not see him, cannot address him, but hears only a voice, which reaches him as from the ground out of the midst of the stir,* of one calling upon the Son of David for help. Jesus comes to a stand and sends *to have him fetched*! They follow the voice and find the man sitting upon the ground. Rise, he calleth thee! they say to him. He throws away his garment, springs up, and presses through the crowd to Jesus. As Jesus sees the man approaching him thus he can have no idea that he is blind!

He has to ask him, therefore, what he wants. The distance, the halt, the sending to fetch him, the nimble approach,—all this Matthew has dropped. He has simplified the situation: Jesus encounters the two blind men on the road and at once addresses them. Only he has retained from the original situation the question, "what is wanted?" —which in Mark is actually necessary, but in Matthew remains unaccountable, for there Jesus must see that he has to do with two blind men!

But if there lay such a distance between Jesus and the blind man, no one could have an idea that he took the monotonous cry about the Son of David as an address to himself! It was just simply an annoying cry, which the bystanders sought in vain to silence. The people attached as little importance to it as to the cries of the demons—if in fact they understood it at all.

The *address* of the beggar was of an entirely different tenor and shows that he no more took Jesus for the Messiah than did the people: "Rabbi, that I may receive my sight." For him, therefore, Jesus was the rabbi from Nazareth.

If one keep this situation in view, it will be seen that the bystanders could in no way get the idea that Jesus here welcomes a messianic acclaim. This, however, was the first sign which he again performed after coming out of his retirement. Thereby he legitimated himself before the Paschal caravan as the Forerunner, for which his adherents in Galilee took him before he suddenly withdrew into solitude in the north. Now the demonstration is let loose, and they prepare for him as the Forerunner the ovation at the entrance into Jerusalem.

In demonstrating the proper character of this occurrence one has to deal with apparently insignificant detail to which not everyone may be inclined to ascribe due importance. In view of this the following points are to be kept in mind:

1. In the representation which assumes the messiahship of Jesus there must come about as of itself a shifting of detail which has the effect of describing a messianic entrance. This is the case with Matthew. There is no evidence of a deliberate purpose on the part of the writer.

2. Mark's delineation shows such originality in comparison with the parallels (one has but to think of the story of the Baptism and the report of the Last Supper) that one cannot easily lay too great weight upon the peculiarity of his account,—especially when it results in so clear and consistent a picture as is here the case.

3. Nothing is accomplished by the assertion that proof has not been brought that it was assuredly a question of an ovation to the Forerunner. For then it remains to demonstrate how it was, that, on the presumption that it was actually an ovation to the Messiah, the transactions in the Jerusalem days make no allusion at all to the presumed messianic pretension and the venal accusers do not appeal to any such claims. What must the Roman procurator have done if a man had marched into the city hailed by the populace as the Son of David?

4. The true historical apprehension is peculiarly difficult for us here because of our notion that the signs and wonders were regarded by the contemporaries as a confirmation of the messiahship of Jesus. In that opinion we share the standpoint upon which the Johannine representation is based. According to the conception of Jesus' contemporaries, however, the Messiah needs no signs, but rather he will be at once manifest in his power! The signs belong on the contrary to the period of the Forerunner!

5. Our translation also has a prejudicial effect. The word ἐρχόμενος denotes in all passages a personality

sharply defined for that time. Hence one must in every case translate it in accord with this perception,—not one time as a substantive [cf. the German Bible] and again (in the story of the ovation) as a verb-form, just as happens to be most convenient. "The Coming One" is the Forerunner, because before the messianic judgment he is to come in the name of God to put everything in order.

We arrive therefore at the conclusion: *Until the confession before the council Jesus was publicly regarded as the Forerunner, as he had been already in Galilee.*

CHAPTER VII

After the Mission of the Twelve. Literary and Historical Problems

1. *The Voyage on the Lake after the Return of the Twelve*

It is exceedingly difficult to gather from the Synoptic accounts a clear picture of the events which happened after the mission of the Twelve. When did the Disciples return? Where did Jesus betake himself during their absence? What sort of success did the Disciples have? What events happened between their return and the departure for the north? Were these events of a sort to account for Jesus' determination to withdraw with them into solitude?

The accounts supply no answer to these questions. Moreover they confront us with another, a purely literary problem. The connection between the several scenes is here extraordinarily broken. It seems almost as if the thread of the narration were here completely lost. Only at the moment of departure for the journey to Jerusalem do the scenes begin to stand again in a clear and natural relationship.

First of all we have to do with two obvious doublettes: the feeding of the multitude and the subsequent journey on the lake (Mk. 6:31, 56; Mk. 8:1, 22). In both instances Jesus is overtaken by the multitude as he lands on a lonely shore after a journey across the lake. Then he returns again to the Galilean village on the west shore. Here in his accustomed field of activity he encounters the

Pharisaic emissaries from Jerusalem. They call him to account. In the series which contains the first account of the feeding of the multitude the question at issue is about hand-washing (Mk. 7:1, 23), in the second case it is the requirement of a sign (Mk. 8:11, 13). The first series concludes with the departure for the north, where in the neighbourhood of Tyre and Sidon he meets the Canaanitish woman (Mk. 7:24, 30). In the second series the journey to Cæsarea Philippi (Mk. 8:27) follows upon his encounter with the Pharisees.

We have here therefore two independent accounts of the same epoch in Jesus's life. In their plan they match one another perfectly, differing only in the choice of the events to be related. These two narrative series are as it were predestinated to be united instead of being placed side by side. It happens that each of the northern journeys, according to the narrative, begins and ends with a sojourn in Galilee. Mk. 7:31: After leaving the region of Tyre he came through Sidon to the Sea of Galilee. Mk. 9:30,33: And they went forth from thence (i. e. from Cæsarea Philippi) and wandered through Galilee and came to Capernaum. At the end of one narrative series one finds oneself again at the beginning of the other. Hence if one connects the one return from the north with the beginning of the other narrative series, one has, superficially viewed, a perfectly natural continuation,—only that Jesus must now, incomprehensibly enough, start back immediately for the north, instead of the return to Galilee being a stage on the journey to Jerusalem! This is the order that was finally followed, but it is only in the second return that the narrative finds a point of attachment for the journey to Jerusalem.

This return movement in both series accounts for the fact that the two narratives, though they are really parallel cycles, are yet attached to one another in chronological sequence. The present text has completed the process of harmonising them. It is not simply that the story of the second feeding of the multitude makes reference to the first in the word "again" (Mk. 8:1): the reconciliation is in fact carried so far that Jesus in one word addressed to the Disciples assumes both miracles (Mk. 8:19, 21)! How far this process was already accomplished in the oral tradition, and how much is to be charged to the account of the final literary composition, is a question which we are no longer in a position to answer.

Only the first cycle is complete. Jesus and his Disciples travel by boat north-east along the coast and return then again to the country of Genezareth (Mk. 6:32, 45, 53).

The second cycle is incomplete and fallen somewhat into disorder. Jesus is back on the west coast after his voyage. Mk. 8:10 ff corresponds with Mk. 6:53 ff and 7:1 ff. Dalmanutha lies on the west coast. But instead of his departing now directly for the north, there comes first another voyage to the east coast (8:13). It is not till they reach Bethsaida that he starts with his Disciples northward (Mk. 8:22, 27). The first cycle on the other hand relates *this voyage to Bethsaida as an episode of the famous coasting voyage and places it immediately after the feeding of the multitude* (Mk. 6:45 ff). And as a matter of fact the second narrative series also shows that this was the original connection. For here, too, as in the first series, the conversation upon landing deals with the foregoing miracle. Mk. 6:52: "For they understood not concerning the loaves, but their heart was hardened." Mk. 8:19, 21: "When I brake the five loaves—when the seven—do ye not yet understand?" It is therefore impossible that between this voyage and the feeding of the multitude all the events were crowded which were enacted upon the west shore. The minds of all are still full of the great event. The new sea journey of the second cycle is nothing else but the original continuation of the voyage to Bethsaida from the scene of the feeding of the multitude.

Therewith the parallelism of the two series is proven. The events follow one another in this order: coasting voyage from the west shore, feeding of the multitude, continuation of the voyage to the north-east, "walking upon the sea" and conversation in the boat, arrival at Bethsaida, return to the region of Genezareth, discussion with the Pharisees, departure with the Disciples to the north.

2. *The Supper by the Seashore*

The Disciples' proclamation of the immediate approach of the Kingdom must have had a great success. A mighty multitude of such as believed the message crowded around Jesus. He had about him a community inspired by the most lively eschatological expectation. They would not let go of him. In order to be alone with his Disciples he embarks in a boat. He meant to withdraw to the north-east shore. But the people, when they learned that he would take himself away, streamed together from all sides and followed him along the beach. Mk. 6:32, 33: "For there were many coming and going, and they had no leisure so much as to eat. And they went away in a boat to a desert place apart. And the people saw them going, and many knew them, and they ran there together on foot from all the cities and outwent them."

They meet him in a lonely region and immediately surround him. The hour comes for the daily meal. In the accounts of the following miracle the meal which they celebrated is preserved to us. *The occasion was a solemn cultus-meal!* After the loaves which he had broken were consecrated by a prayer of thanksgiving Jesus has them distributed to the multitude by his Disciples. Except for the addition of the two parables ["My body—my blood"] we have absolutely the same solemn ceremony at the Last Supper. There he personally distributed the food to his table-companions. The description of the distribution of the bread in the two cases corresponds perfectly. Mk. 6:41: He took the loaves, and looking up to heaven, he blessed them, and he gave to the Disciples to set before them. Mk. 14:22: He took a loaf, and when he had blessed, he brake it, and gave to them.

Hence the *solemn act of distribution* constitutes the essence, as well of that meal by the seashore, as of the last meal with his Disciples. The "Lord's Supper" is a name appropriate to both, for that meal by the sea also took place at the evening hour. Mk. 6:35: And when the day was now far spent his Disciples came to him, etc. Here the table-company is composed of the great multitude of believers in the Kingdom: at the Last Supper it was limited to the circle of the Disciples. *The celebration, however, was the same.*

The story of this event has been distorted into a miracle: the cultus-meal which Jesus improvised by the seashore has been represented as a hearty and filling supper. That the scanty provision which was at hand, the food designed for himself and his Disciples, was solemnly distributed to the people is historic. That this meal took the place of the evening repast likewise corresponds with the fact. But that through a supernatural process the multitude was *filled* by it,—that belongs to the miraculous character which the later age ascribed to the celebration because its significance could not be apprehended.

The historical procedure is the following: The Disciples ask Jesus to send the people away that they may be fed. For him, however, it is not an appropriate moment to think of an earthly meal and so to disperse, for the hour is near when they shall all be gathered about him at the messianic banquet. Hence he would not have them go yet, but before he dismisses them he commands them to recline as at table. In place of the full meal he introduces a ceremonial meal, in which the satisfaction of earthly appetite has no part, so that the food intended for himself and his Disciples sufficed for all.

Neither the Disciples nor the multitude understand what goes on. As Jesus afterwards in the boat directs the conversation to the significance of the meal—this alone can be the historical meaning of the obscure intimations of Mk. 6:52 and Mk. 8:14, 21—it appears that the Disciples have understood nothing.

He celebrated, therefore, a sacred cultus-meal the meaning of which was clear to him alone. He did not count it necessary to explain to them the meaning of the ceremony. The memory, however, of that mysterious supper on the lonely seashore lived on vividly in the tradition and grew to the account of the miraculous feeding. Wherein did the solemnity of this distribution consist for Jesus? The gathering at the feast is of an eschatological character. The people that gathered about him by the seaside were awaiting with him the dawn of the Kingdom. In replacing now the customary full meal with a sacred ceremonial meal, at which he distributed food with thanksgiving to God, he acted at the prompting of his messianic consciousness. *As one who knew himself to be the Messiah, and would be manifested to them as such at the imminent dawn of the Kingdom, he distributes, to those whom he expects soon to join him at the messianic banquet, sacred food, as though he would give them therewith an earnest of their participation in that future solemnity.* The time for earthly meals is passed: hence he celebrates with them a foretaste of the messianic banquet. They, however, understood it not, for they could not guess that he who distributed to them such consecrated eucharistic food was conscious of being the Messiah and acted as such.

In this connection there falls a light upon the nature of the Last Supper at Jerusalem. There the Disciples represented the community of believers in the Kingdom. In the course of that last meal Jesus distributed to them with a word of thanksgiving food and drink. But now they know what he assumes to be: he had disclosed to them the secret of his messiahship. From this they are able to divine in his distribution the reference to the messianic banquet. He himself gave this significance to his action in the fact that he concluded the ceremony with a hint of their proximate reunion when he should drink the wine new with them in his Father's Kingdom!

The supper by the seaside and the supper at Jerusalem therefore correspond completely, except that in the latter Jesus signified to his Disciples the nature of the ceremony and at the same time expresses the thought of the Passion in the two parables ["My body—my blood"]. The cultus-meal was the same: a foretaste of the messianic banquet in the circle of the fellowship of the believers in the Kingdom. *Now for the first time one is able to understand how the nature of the Last Supper can be independent of the two parables.*

3. *The Week at Bethsaida*

During the ceremony Jesus was deeply moved. For this reason he urged immediate departure and dismissed the people. He himself withdrew to a mountain in order to be alone in prayer. On the beach at Bethsaida, whither he had charged them to row, he again met his Disciples. They, battling with wind and wave, had the illusion that a supernatural apparition approached them as they descried his figure on the beach. They still were so much under the influence of the impression lately made upon them by the mighty personality who with mysterious majesty had distributed to the multitude sacred food and then had suddenly broken off the ceremony (Mk. 6:45, 52).

Whither had he sent away the multitude? What did they do at Bethsaida? How long did they stay there? Our text merely recounts that they returned again to Genezareth.

At this point, however, we encounter a difficult literary problem, in the Synoptical narrative of the period immediately preceding the departure for Jerusalem (Mk. 9:30). According to Mk. 8:27, 33, Jesus is now alone with his Disciples far away in the north, in heathen territory,—from which point also he sets out on the rapid march through Galilee to Jerusalem (Mk. 9:30 ff): "And they went forth from thence and passed through Galilee, and he would not that any man should know it." Between the disclosure of his messiahship and this departure there intervenes only one scene (Mk. 8:34; 9:29), where he appears surrounded by a great multitude of people. In company with the three intimate Disciples he leaves the multitude, only to return to them shortly again. It is nowhere recounted how this multitude suddenly gets to him in heathen territory. And just as little are we informed how it leaves him again, so that (according to Mk. 9:30 ff) he can march through Galilee alone with his Disciples and unrecognised.

But it is not only the multitude that appears unexpectedly: the whole scenery also is altered. One finds oneself in a familiar region, for Jesus enters with his Disciples "into the house," while the people stay without (Mk. 9:28)!

The literary context in which the section stands is absolutely impossible, for this cannot have been enacted in *heathen territory,* but only in *Galilee*! But as Jesus subsequently had only a fleeting contact with Galilee, passing through it incognito, this piece belongs in the Galilean period *before the departure for the north, and more precisely, at the time of the return of the Disciples,* for it is then that he was constantly surrounded by a throng of people and was seeking to be in solitude with his Disciples!

The situation, however may confidently be defined with still greater exactness. Jesus dwelt in a village (Mk. 9:28) in the neighbourhood of which there was a mountain to which he betook himself with the three Disciples (Mk. 9:2). All this agrees, however, most certainly with the sojourn in *Bethsaida.* The mountain which he seeks with the Three is *the mountain on the north shore of the lake where he prayed in the night when he came to Bethsaida!*

The passage Mk. 8:34; 9:29 belongs therefore in the days at Bethsaida! It is no longer possible to make out by what process it came into the present impossible context. The adoption of the present order may have been prompted in part by the consideration that the impressive word about the obligation of following Jesus in suffering (Mk. 8:34; 9:1) seemed to form a most natural conclusion to the prediction of the Passion at Cæsarea Philippi (Mk. 8:31, 33).

Moreover the transformation of the account of Jesus meeting his Disciples at their landing into a miracle made it difficult to effect a natural connection with the events which occurred the following morning. And yet Mk. 8:34 ff may fairly be said to imply such measures as were adopted the evening before (Mk. 6:45, 47). Jesus had dismissed the people, had himself retired to solitude, and while it was yet night had overtaken his Disciples at Bethsaida, where they found lodging in a house (Mk. 9:28). The next day he calls the people about him with the Disciples (Mk. 8:34) and speaks to them about the requirement of self-denial on the part of his followers, readiness to endure shame, scorn, ridicule, rather than prove untrue to him. This conduct is justified by the nearness of the coming of the Son of Man, who will perform judgment in the person of Jesus.

This admonition concludes with a word about "the coming of the Kingdom of God with power," *i.e.* the eschatological realisation of it. In its present form it is toned down: some of them that stand by shall not taste of death till that moment arrive. As the conclusion of this address, however, it must have run: Ye who stand here shall soon experience the great moment of the mighty dawn of the Kingdom of God! Thus this earnest address at Bethsaida reflects the expectations which stirred Jesus and the throng about him.

Six days after that address at Bethsaida Jesus took with him the Three and led them to the mountain where he had prayed in solitude at evening after the great cultus-meal in common. At their return they find the other Disciples surrounded by the people. In spite of the authority over demons of which they had made proof during their progress through the cities of Israel, they were now not able to master a demoniac boy who was brought to them. Jesus takes the father and boy apart. The very moment that the people come running together (Mk. 9:25, 27) the crisis begins, after which Jesus takes by the hand the lad, who was lying as dead, and raises him up.

This passage, therefore, which has been wrested so

strangely out of its connection, contains a striking account of the first and last days of the week which Jesus passed in Bethsaida between the return of the Disciples and the departure for the north.

It will now be perfectly clear how unhistoric is the view that Jesus left Galilee in consequence of growing opposition and spreading defection. On the contrary, this is the period of his highest triumph. A multitude of people with faith in the Kingdom thronged him and pursued him everywhere. Hardly has he landed upon the west coast but they are already there. Their number has grown still greater and increases more and more (Mk. 6:53, 56). That they deserted him, that they even showed the least motion of doubt or defection, the texts give no intimation. *It was not the people that deserted Jesus but Jesus that deserted the people.*

This he did, not out of any fear of the emissaries from Jerusalem, but only as carrying out what he already had in mind since the return of the Disciples. He wishes to be alone. The people had defeated this aim by following him along the shore as he sailed. When he had returned to the west coast he found himself again surrounded. Because he felt it absolutely necessary to be alone with the Disciples, and because he was not able to effect this purpose in Galilee, for this cause he suddenly vanished and betook himself into heathen territory. *The journey into the north country is not a flight, rather it has the same motive as the voyage on the lake.*

CHAPTER VIII

The Secret of Messiahship

1. *From the Mount of Transfiguration to Cæsarea Philippi*

Coming after Cæsarea Philippi the Transfiguration is an obscure episode devoid of historical significance. The Three learn no more about Jesus than Peter had already confessed in the presence of the Twelve and Jesus himself had confirmed. Thus the whole section is plainly an intrusion: the apotheosis and obscure dialogue have no historical significance.

If, however, as has been proved above by literary evidence, this scene was enacted some weeks after the mission of the Twelve and *before* Cæsarea Philippi—not upon the mountain of the legend, but on the mountain in the lonely region by the seashore near Bethsaida,—then we behold an idle addendum transformed at one stroke into a Galilean occurrence of far reaching historical importance, which explains the scene at Cæsarea Philippi, and not vice versa. What we call the Transfiguration is in reality nothing else but the revelation of the secret of messiahship to the Three. A few weeks later comes then its disclosure to the Twelve.

This revelation to the Three is handed down to us in the form of a miracle-tale. It has undergone the same transformation as have all the incidents of that voyage along the north coast. The scene on the mountain, like the feeding of the multitude and the encounter of Jesus with his disciples at dusk, bears evident marks of the intense eschatological excitement of the moment. For this reason the historical facts are no longer clear in detail. There appear unto them Moses and Elijah, the two characters most prominently associated with the expectation of the last times. To what extent may ecstatic conditions, and perhaps glossolalia, have contributed to this experience? The present form of the story permits us to infer something of the sort (Mk. 9:2–6). Does the voice out of the cloud (Mk. 9:7, "This is my beloved Son, hear ye him") repeat in some sort Jesus' experience at his baptism?

There is in fact an inward connection between the Baptism and the Transfiguration. In both cases a condition of ecstasy accompanies the revelation of the secret of Jesus' person. The first time the revelation was for him alone; here the Disciples also share it. It is not clear to what extent they themselves were transported by the experience. So much is sure, that in a dazed condition, out of which they awake only at the end of the scene (Mk. 9:8), the figure of Jesus appears to them illuminated by a supernatural light and glory, and a voice intimates that he is the Son of God. The occurrence can be explained only as the outcome of great eschatological excitement.

It is remarkable that the revelation of the secret of Jesus' messiahship appears always to be connected with such conditions. At Pentecost, when Peter openly proclaimed Jesus as the Christ, we have an example of glossolalia. Peter, to be sure, had already had a taste of such an experience as the revelation was made to him on the mountain near Bethsaida. Paul also was in a state of ecstasy when he heard the voice before the Damascus gate.

It has been shown above that no one could conclude from Jesus' speech or behaviour that he regards himself as the Messiah. Properly the question is not, how the people could remain ignorant of Jesus' messianic claim, but how Peter at Cæsarea Philippi and the High Priest at the trial could come into possession of this secret.

The Transfiguration answers the first question. Peter knew that Jesus is the "Son of God" through the revelation which he in common with the two other Disciples received on the mountain near Bethsaida. For this reason he answered the question with such confidence (Mk. 8:29). The text of St. Matthew's Gospel records an additional saying of Jesus which seems to allude to the very experience in which this knowledge was supernaturally imparted to Peter: "Blessed art thou, Simon Bar-Jonah: for flesh and blood hath not revealed it unto thee, but my Father which is in heaven" (Mt. 16:17).

Moreover, the scene which follows upon Peter's answer clearly has to do with a secret common to him and to Jesus. When Jesus disclosed that he must die in Jerusalem Peter turns upon him impetuously, takes him apart, and speaks to him in excited tones. As Jesus sees that the other Disciples are attentive he abruptly turns away from Peter with a sharp word, calling him the Tempter, who minds not the things of God but the things of men (Mk. 8:32, 33).

Why this agitation of Peter over Jesus' disclosure about the fatal journey to Jerusalem? Because it comes as a new factor, above and beyond what was disclosed on the mountain near Bethsaida. About that experience he dare not speak in the presence of the other Disciples, because Jesus had forbidden it. For this reason he takes Jesus apart. Jesus, however, seeing that the other Disciples are listening, cannot explain matters to him, and so with passionate abruptness enjoins silence.

Only the connection with the foregoing Transfiguration explains the characteristic traits of the scene at Cæsarea Philippi. Psychological observations about the quick apprehension and lively temperament of Peter—the common expedients of modern interpretation—do not in fact begin to explain why he alone should arrive with such confidence at the knowledge of Jesus' messiahship, only to fall a moment later into such misunderstanding that he gets into an excited dispute with Jesus. Why do they both go apart together? Why, instead of instructing him, does Jesus leave him there with a hard word of rebuke?

Taken by itself the whole scene at Cæsarea Philippi is an enigma. If, however, we assume that the Transfiguration preceded it, the enigma is solved and the scene is illuminated down to the smallest details. The revelation to the Twelve was preceded by the disclosure to the Three of the secret of Jesus' messiahship.

2. *The Futuristic Character of Jesus' Messiahship*

Meanwhile the revelation of the secret of his messiahship alters nothing in the behaviour of the Disciples to Jesus. They do not sink before him in the dust as if now the man whom they had known was become a superhuman being. They only manifest in consequence of this revelation a certain awe. They dare not interrogate him when they fail to understand his words (Mk. 9:32), and as they company with him they appear to be aware that he carries within him a great secret.

Are we to imagine then that after this revelation of his secret Jesus was henceforth regarded by his disciples as the Messiah? No, *not yet* was he the Messiah. It must constantly be kept in mind that the Kingdom and the Messiah are correlative terms which belong inseparably together. Now if the Kingdom was not yet come, neither was the Messiah. Jesus' disclosure had reference to the time of the dawning of the Kingdom. When that hour shall strike, then shall he appear as Messiah, then shall his messiahship be revealed in glory. Such was the secret which he solemnly made known to his disciples.

Jesus' messiahship was a secret, not merely because he had forbidden it to be spoken, but in its very nature it was a secret, inasmuch as it could be realised only at a definite time in the future. It was a conception which could be formulated fully only in his own consciousness. Wherefore the people could not understand it—and need not know anything about it. It was enough if by his word and his signs he might convert them to faith in the nearness of the kingdom, for with the coming of the Kingdom his messiahship would be manifest.

It is almost impossible to express in modern terms the consciousness of messiahship which Jesus imparted as a secret to his Disciples. Whether we describe it as an identity between him and the Son of Man who is to appear, whether we express it as a continuity which unites both personalities, or think of it as virtually a pre-existent messiahship,—none of these modern conceptions can render the consciousness of Jesus as the Disciples understood it.

What we lack is the "Now and Then" which dominated their thinking and which explains a curious duality of consciousness that was characteristic of them. What we might call identity, continuity, and potentiality was in their mind confounded in a conception which quite eludes our grasp. Every person figured himself in two entirely different states, according as he thought of himself now, in the pre-messianic age, or then in the messianic. Expressions which we interpret only in accordance with our unity of consciousness, they referred as a matter of course to the double consciousness familiar to them. Therefore when Jesus revealed to them the secret of his messiahship, that did not mean to them that he *is* the Messiah, as we moderns must understand it; rather it signified for them that their Lord and Master was the one who in the messianic age would be revealed as Messiah.

They think of themselves also in terms of this double consciousness. As often as Jesus made known to them the necessity of his suffering before entering upon his rule they questioned within themselves what manner of persons they should be in the coming age. Wherefore, following upon the prophecies of the Passion we find rivalry among the Disciples as to which shall be the greatest in the Kingdom, or to whom shall be accorded the seats of honour on either side of the throne. In the meanwhile, however, they remain what they are, and Jesus remains what he is, their Teacher and Master. The sons of Zebedee address him as "Master" (Mk. 10:35). As Teacher they expect him to give promise and assurance of what shall come to pass when the Kingdom dawns and his messiahship is revealed.

In this sense, then, Jesus' messianic consciousness is futuristic. There was nothing strange in this either for him or for his Disciples. On the contrary, it corresponded exactly to the Jewish conception of the hidden life and labour of the Messiah.[1] The course of Jesus' earthly life preceded his messiahship in glory. The Messiah in his earthly estate must live and labour unrecognised, he must teach, and through deed and suffering he must be made perfect in righteousness. Not till then shall the messianic age dawn with the Last Judgment and the establishment of the Kingdom. The Messiah must come from the north. Jesus' march from Cæsarea Philippi to Jerusalem was the progress of the unrecognised Messiah to his triumph in glory.

[1] Cf. Weber: *System der altsynagogalen Theologie,* 1880, pp. 342–446.

Thus in the midst of the messianic expectation of his people stood Jesus as the Messiah that is to be. He dare not reveal himself to them, for the season of his hidden labour was not yet over. Hence he preached the near approach of the Kingdom of God.

It was this futuristic consciousness of messiahship which prompted Jesus in the Temple to touch upon the messianic dogma of the Scribes, as though he would call their attention to the secret which lurks behind it. The Pharisees say, "The Messiah is David's Son;" but David calls him his Lord. How can he still be his Son (Mk. 12:35–37)?

The Messiah is David's Son—that is, subordinate to him—since in this era he is born of human parentage and lives and labours in obscurity. David's Lord, because at the dawn of the coming era he will be revealed as Christ in glory. Jesus has no notion of impeaching the pharisaic dogma. It is correct, the Scripture so teaches. Only, the Pharisees themselves cannot properly interpret their dogma, and so cannot explain how the Messiah can be in one instance David's Son and in another, David's Lord.

This saying of Jesus to the people in the Temple—(only Matthew has made of it an embarrassing polemic)—is on a line with his utterance about the Baptist. Whoever could apprehend with what authority John baptised—that is, with the power and authority of Elijah,—whoever could understand how the Messiah could be in one instance David's son, in another David's Lord,—he must know also who *he* is that so speaks. He that hath ears to hear, let him hear!

3. *The Son of Man and the Futuristic Character of Jesus' Messiahship*

The expression "Son of David" contains an enigma.

Therefore Jesus never used it in speaking of his messiahship, but always refers to himself as the "Son of Man." Consequently this designation must have been peculiarly apt as a rendering of his messianic consciousness.

It is evident that he chose this term deliberately. Every other messianic designation that is applied to him he corrects and interprets by "Son of Man."

As they descend from the mountain where the Disciples had come to recognise him as the Son of God he speaks of himself as the "Son of Man" (Mk. 9:7–9).

Peter proclaimed him before the others as "the Anointed one" (Mk. 8:29). Jesus immediately proceeds to instruct them about the fate of the "Son of Man" (Mk. 8:31).

"Art thou the Christ the Son of the Blessed?" the High Priest asked him (Mk. 14:61). "Ye shall see the Son of Man sitting at the right hand of power and coming with the clouds of heaven," is Jesus' answer. That signifies, *Yes*. The same expression occurs in the second and in the third prophecy of the Passion (Mk. 9:30–32; 10:32–34) and in the saying about serving (Mk. 10:45).

The messianic title "Son of Man" is futuristic in character. It refers to the moment in which the Messiah shall come upon the clouds of heaven for judgment. From the beginning this was the sense in which Jesus had used the expression, whether in speaking to the people or to the Disciples. In sending out his Apostles he warned them of the impending approach of the day of the Son of Man (Mt. 10:23). He spoke to the people of the coming of the Son of Man as an exhortation to be faithful to him, Jesus (Mk. 8:38).

Withal, he and the Son of Man remain for the people and for the Disciples two entirely distinct personalities. The one is a terrestrial, the other a celestial figure; the one belongs to the age that now is, the other to the messianic period. Between the two there exists solidarity, inasmuch as the Son of Man will intervene in behalf of such as have ranged themselves on the side of Jesus, the herald of his coming.

These are the passages one must take as the point of departure in order to understand the significance of this expression in Jesus' mouth. Jesus and the Son of Man are different persons for such as do not know his secret. They, however, to whom he has revealed his secret are aware of a personal connection between the two. Jesus it is who at the messianic day shall appear as the Son of Man. The revelation at Cæsarea Philippi consists in this, that Jesus reveals to his Disciples in what personal relationship he stands to the coming Son of Man. As the one who is to be the Son of Man he can confirm Peter's confession of him as the Messiah. His reply to the High Priest is affirmative in the same sense. He is the Messiah—that they will see when he appears as the Son of Man upon the clouds of heaven.

"Son of Man" is accordingly the adequate expression of his messiahship, so long as he, in this earthly æon as Jesus of Nazareth, has occasion to refer to his future dignity. Hence when he speaks to the Disciples about himself as the Son of Man he assumes this duality of consciousness. "The Son of Man must suffer and will then rise from the dead:" that is to say, "As the one who is to be Son of Man at the resurrection of the dead I must suffer." To the same effect we must understand the word about serving: As the one who in the character of the Son of Man is destined to the highest rule I must now humble myself to the lowliest service (Mk. 10:45). Therefore he says when they come to arrest him: The hour is come in the which he who is to be the Son of Man must be delivered into the hands of sinners (Mk. 14:21, 41).

The problem about the Son of Man is herewith elucidated. It was not an expression which Jesus commonly used to describe himself, but a solemn title which he adopted when in the great moments of his life he spoke about himself to the initiated as the future Messiah, while before the others he spoke of the Son of Man as a personality distinct from himself. In all cases, however, the context shows that he is speaking of one who is yet to come, for in all these passages mention is made either of the Resurrection or of the appearing upon the clouds of heaven. The philological objections do not therefore apply here. Initiated and uninitiated must understand from the situation that he is speaking of a definite personality of the future,—and not of man in general, even though the expression in both cases would be the same.

The case is entirely different with another set of passages where the expression occurs arbitrarily as a pure self-designation, a roundabout way of saying "I." Here all critical and philological objections are thoroughly in place.

Mt. 8:20—The Son of Man hath not where to lay his head.

Mt. 11:19—The Son of Man is come eating and drinking (in contrast to the Baptist).

Mt. 12:32—Blasphemy against the Holy Spirit is a worse crime than speaking evil of the Son of Man.

Mt. 12:40—The Son of Man will be three days in the earth, like Jonah in the belly of the fish.

Mt. 13:37, 41—The Son of Man is the Sower; the Son of Man is the lord of the reapers.

Mt. 16:13—Who do the people say that the Son of Man is?

Here the expression is philologically impossible. For if Jesus had so used it, his hearers must simply have understood him to mean "man." There is nothing here to indicate that the word is meant to express a future messianic dignity! Here in fact he designates by it his actual present condition! But "Son of Man" is a messianic title of futuristic character, since it always suggests a coming upon the clouds, according to Daniel 7:13, 14. Furthermore, in all of these passages the Disciples are as yet ignorant of Jesus' secret. For them the Son of Man is still an entirely distinct person. The unity of the subject is still completely unknown to them. Therefore they were not in a position to understand that by this term he refers to himself, but they must refer everything to that Son of Man of whose coming he also spoke elsewhere. Therewith, however, the passages would be meaningless, for they imply that Jesus is thus speaking of himself.

Historically and philologically it is therefore impossible that Jesus could have employed the expression as a purposeless and matter of course self-designation. Even as a self-designation referable to the future messianic dignity that was to be his, only they could understand it who knew his secret. Hence all the passages are unhistorical in which, *previous to Cæsarea Philippi* (or, for the Three, previous to the Transfiguration), he designates *himself* as Son of Man. Only those in that period are historical in which he speaks of the Son of Man as a figure yet to come, not identical with himself (Mt. 10:23 and Mk. 8:38). The passages cited above, in which the expression is used without its proper significance as a mere self-designation, are therefore not historical, but are comprehensible only as the result of a literary process. How does it come about that a later period of Gospel composition regarded this expression as "Jesus' self-designation"?

This was due to a shifting of the perspective. It is observable from the moment when men began to write the history of Jesus upon the assumption that on earth he was already the Messiah. From that time on men lost consciousness of the fact that for the earthly existence of Jesus his very messiahship was something future, and that by the very expression Son of Man he designated himself as the future Messiah. Since, then, it was an historic fact that he spoke of himself as the Son of Man, the writers appropriated this emphatic term and without suspecting that it was appropriate only in certain sayings and in definite situations, they employed it indifferently in any passage where Jesus spoke of himself,—and thereby created these philological and historical impossibilities.

This erroneous use was due therefore to a literary development of markedly secondary character. In this respect it was like the unhistorical use of the expression "Son of David" by Matthew. It agrees thereto that the "Son of Man" passages here in question belong likewise to a secondary stratum of St. Matthew's Gospel.

What chiefly reveals their secondary character is: the transformation of the simple question asked at Cæsarea Philippi (Mt. 16:13); the application of the parable of the sower (Mt. 13:37, 41); and the false interpretation of the saying about Jonah (Mt. 12:40).

No less secondary is the formulation of the speech about the sin against the Holy Ghost, where a contrast is drawn between blasphemy against the Holy Ghost and against the Son of Man (Mt. 22:32), whereas in Jesus' thought both came to the same thing, since it was a question of conscious hardening against the power of the coming Kingdom which worked in him. In the passages Mt. 8:20 and Mt. 11:19 the expression is arbitrarily used, for Jesus merely wishes to say: *I* have nowhere to lay my head; and, *I* eat and drink, in contrast to the ascetic practice of the Baptist.

It is quite a different case which is presented by the two unhistorical "Son of Man" passages in St. Mark's Gospel.

Mk. 2:10—The Son of Man hath authority to forgive sins upon earth.
Mk. 2:28—The Son of Man is lord of the Sabbath.

The secondary character appears in the fact that Jesus is supposed to have used the expression here as a self-designation. The historical fact is that he used it in that connection in the third person, referring either to the Son of Man as an eschatological figure, or to man in general. In either case it makes sense.

1. Man as such can by works of healing declare the forgiveness of sins upon earth.

Man as man is lord of the Sabbath.

2. In view of the coming of the Son of Man forgiveness of sins is already available, as the works of healing show.

In view of the coming of the Son of Man a higher factor already emerges to modify the legalistic observance of the Sabbath.

The Law yields to something higher. The case of David shows it.

However one may explain these passages, one thing is clear: the expression did actually occur here and did somehow modify Jesus' statement. The only secondary trait appears in the use of the expression as a self-designation, whereas in fact Jesus spoke of man in general or of the Son of Man. These passages, therefore, are on the threshold between the historical and the literary-unhistorical use of the name "Son of Man."

We can now understand the peculiar difficulty of the "Son of Man" problem. Hitherto, the deeper the investigation went, so much the further the solution seemed to recede. This was due to the fact that no amount of reflection could effect the separation of passages of such unequal worth. Thus the literary and historical sides of the problem remained confounded with one another. The moment, however, the discovery is made, from the study of Jesus' messianic consciousness, that the expression Son of Man is the only one by which he could utter the secret of his future dignity, the separation is given. All those passages are historical which show the influence of the apocalyptic reference to the Son of Man in Daniel: all are unhistorical in which such is not the case. At the same time the shifting of the perspective explains why for writers of a later generation this expression in Jesus' mouth could have only the significance of an arbitrary self-designation, appropriate in all situations where he spoke of himself.

Finally, the last enigma is also solved. Why does the expression disappear from the language of the primitive Church? Why does no one (with exception of Acts 7:56) designate the Messiah by the title Son of Man, notwithstanding that Jesus had used it exclusively to indicate his dignity? This is due to the fact that "Son of Man" was the messianic expression for a clearly defined episode of the messianic drama. The Messiah was the Son of Man in the moment of his manifestation upon the clouds of heaven to reign in judgment over the world. Jesus thought exclusively of that moment, since only from that moment on was he for men the Messiah. The primitive Church, however, seeing that a transitional period intervened, beheld Jesus as the Messiah in heaven above at the right hand of God. He was already the Messiah and did not have to become such at the moment of the appearing of the Son of Man. Because the perspective was shifted here also, one used the general expression "Messiah" instead of the title "Son of Man" which pointed to a particular scene.

Jesus would have expressed himself inaccurately had he said, I am the Messiah,—for that he was to be only when he appeared in glory as the Son of Man.

The primitive Church would have expressed itself inaccurately had it said, Jesus is the Son of Man,—for after the Resurrection he was the Messiah at the right hand of God, whose coming as Son of Man the Church expected.

4. *The Resurrection of the Dead and the Futuristic Character of Jesus' Messiahship*

What is the significance of the resurrection-prophecies? It seems to us hard to admit that Jesus could have foretold so precisely an event of that sort. It seems much more plausible to suppose that general utterances of his about a glory that awaited him were editorially transformed *ex eventu* into predictions of the Resurrection.

Such criticism is in place so long as one holds the view that the prophecy of the Resurrection referred to an isolated event in the personal history of Jesus. So it appears, however, only to our modern consciousness, because we think uneschatologically even in the matter of the Resurrection. For Jesus and his Disciples, on the other hand, the Resurrection which he spoke about had an entirely different significance. It was a messianic event which signified the dawn of the full glory that was to come. We must eliminate from the Resurrection predicted by Jesus all modern notions suggestive of an apotheosis. The contemporary consciousness understood this "Restoration" (Acts 3:21) as a revelation of Jesus' messiahship at the dawn of the Kingdom. Therefore when Jesus spoke of his resurrection the Disciples thought of the great messianic Resurrection in which he as the Messiah would be raised from the dead.

The conversation during the descent from the mountain of Transfiguration is decisive on this point. Jesus spoke then for the first time to his most intimate disciples of "the resurrection of the Son of Man from the dead" (Mk. 9:9). They, however, were quite unable to think of "the resurrection of the Son of man" apart from the messianic Resurrection. Their attention was entirely occupied with the messianic event which Jesus' words suggested to them. They question therefore among themselves about the Resurrection of the dead. What should that mean (Mk. 9:10)? That is to say, the conditions thereof, so far as they can see, are not yet fulfilled. Elijah is not yet come (Mk. 9:11). Jesus puts their minds at rest with the hint that Elijah had already appeared though men did not recognise him. He means the Baptist (Mk. 9:12, 13).

This conversation, in which otherwise it is impossible to detect at all any reasonable sequence of thought, becomes perfectly transparent and natural the moment it is noticed how the Disciples are unable to think of the resurrection which Jesus' words suggest except in the same thought with the general messianic Resurrection. Therefore this talk during the descent from the mountain throws a clear light upon Jesus' later prophecies of his Passion and Resurrection, because we are here in a position to observe the thoughts and questions which these words awaken in the hearts of the Disciples. Moreover this "resurrection prophecy" lacks the mention of the three days which furnishes precisely the occasion for the critical attitude toward the subsequent prophecies of the Passion. In this respect the prediction during the descent agrees thoroughly with the last utterance before the High Priest.

Both lack the definite indication of the time when the Resurrection or the appearing upon the clouds of heaven shall take place. In the messianic event both correspond chronologically: resurrection and coming on the clouds signify only the revelation of Jesus' messiahship on the great Resurrection Day.

This expectation of the eschatological Resurrection of the dead ruled the consciousness of Jesus and his contemporaries. He assumes it in his discourses at Jerusalem. Expectation of the Kingdom and belief in the approaching Resurrection of the dead belong together. It is, as we have already observed, an error in perspective to represent Jesus' thought in regard to the coming Kingdom as directed toward the future as if it had to do with subsequent generations. So the modern mind thinks. It was just the opposite with Jesus. The Kingdom had to do with the past generations. They rise up to meet the Judgment which inaugurates the Kingdom.

The Resurrection of the dead is the condition precedent to the establishment of the Kingdom. Through it all generations of the world are lifted out of their temporal sequence and placed before God's judgment as contemporaries. For example, such a parable even as that of the Lord's Vineyard requires the assumption of the Resurrection of the dead (Mk. 12:1–12). The whole history of Israel is there described in the conduct of the husbandmen. Jesus speaks of the generations of Israel from the days of the Prophets unto the people then present to whom his warning is addressed. The parable, however, pictures only one generation, because when it is a question of the Judgment, the whole people in its consecutive generations appears before God as one collective whole,—which means that it is raised up as a whole from the dead.

In the same way it is to be explained that the people

of Sodom of a generation long gone by are assured of a more tolerable fate than the present inhabitants of Capernaum (Mt. 11:23, 24).

Those who believed in the coming of the Kingdom believed also in the approaching Resurrection of the dead. Wherefore the attack of the Sadducees was directed precisely against this point. Jesus' reply to them, that "when they shall rise from the dead they neither marry nor are given in marriage, but are as the angels in heaven" (Mk. 12:25), is to be understood as descriptive of conditions in the Kingdom of heaven, into which they enter through the Resurrection from the dead.

The "Resurrection of the dead" was, in fine, only the mode in which the transformation of the whole form of existence was accomplished upon those who had already succumbed to death. By the coming of the Kingdom of God, however, the earthly form of existence in general must be raised to another and an incomparably higher estate. From this point of view, those also are to experience a "resurrection" who before the great Event have not succumbed to death; for by a higher power their mode of existence, too, will suddenly be transformed into another, which they will then share with those that have been awakened from death. In comparison with this new form of existence the foregoing condition is a matter of indifference. It is all one whether from our earthly existence or from the sleep of death we pass into the messianic mode of being. In comparison with the latter all being is "death." It alone is "life."

Wherefore, to the living, Jesus speaks of the way that leadeth unto "life" (Mt. 7:14). He counsels men rather to part with a member of the body, when "life" is in question, than to fail of gaining through the Resurrection a part in the messianic existence (Mt. 18:8, 9). The rich young man asks what he must do "to inherit eternal life." Jesus is very sorrowful when he will not follow the counsel given him, because it is so hard for a rich man "to enter into the Kingdom of heaven" (Mk. 10:17, 25).

This disparagement of the earthly form of existence goes to the length of sacrificing altogether the earthly life for the sake of full assurance of life in the coming age. Hence, with the exhortation to follow him in suffering and reproach, Jesus declares that "whosoever would save his life shall lose it." That is to say, Whosoever, through anxiety about his earthly existence, makes himself unworthy that the Son of Man intervene for him before God, forfeits thereby the messianic life which commences with the Resurrection (Mk. 8:35).

When the Kingdom dawns it is all one whether we exist in a living or in a dead body. It is only with this persuasion that a man can meet persecution boldly. Wherefore Jesus says to the Apostles as he sends them forth: Be not afraid of them which kill the body but are not able to kill the "soul," but fear him who hath power to destroy both "soul" and body in hell (Mt. 10:28).

St. Paul furnishes a classical instance of this same connection between the eschatological expectation of the early Church and the Resurrection of the dead (I Cor. 15:50–54). What we have here is not a specifically Pauline thought, but a primitive Christian conception to which Jesus had already given utterance. Flesh and blood, whether quick or dead, can in no wise have part in the Kingdom. Therefore when the hour strikes and the dead are raised incorruptible, the living also shall be changed, putting on incorruption and immortality.

The Resurrection of the dead is the bridge from the "Now" to the "Then." It accounts for the duality of consciousness. Hence when Jesus spoke of his resurrection the Disciples correlated this word with the great context. It signified for them the general Resurrection in which they too would arise in the form of existence appropriate to the Kingdom of God. True, they expected his resurrection,—not, however, as the "Easter event," but as the dawn of the messianic Kingdom. Jesus was to be revealed as the risen Christ when he should come as Son of Man upon the clouds of heaven to usher in the messianic day.

For our feeling, the death of Jesus is related to the Resurrection as a discord in music to its resolution. Owing to the disparagement of every form of existence prior to the messianic age, a much weaker accent, for the Disciples lay upon the death. What they conceived was an endless, eternal accord following upon a brief earthly prelude.

Where we see a juxtaposition of messianic claim, Passion prediction, and Resurrection prophecy, the Disciples perceived a much stricter connection of thought. They beheld all in a messianic light. Hence they did not draw from Jesus' words three separate conclusions: (1) that he was the Messiah; (2) that he must suffer and die; (3) that he would rise from the dead. Rather, the impression they received was this: Our master will after his death, at the Resurrection, be revealed as the Son of Man. At the same time they question within themselves what sort of persons they then will be and what office and dignity will fall to their lot in the new existence.

It can thus be explained why their messianic conception was not completely overthrown by the notion of "the suffering and dying Messiah." Jesus had revealed to them neither the suffering, nor the dying, nor the risen Christ; but he spoke to them of the Son of Man who was due to appear, and revealed to them that it was he who should come in that character when he had perfected himself by suffering here below.

It can never be emphasised enough that in this respect

Jesus' messiahship was completely in line with the popular conception. The tragedy of his life is not to be accounted for by the incompatibility of his notion of messiahship and the general expectation, so that only conflicts could ensue which must bring about his death. This conception first appears in the Fourth Gospel. The historical Jesus laid claim to messiahship only from the moment of the Resurrection.

This view of Jesus' messianic disclosures in the early Synoptic tradition is absolutely required by the conception of the primitive Church. The primitive Church assumes that Jesus' messianic consciousness was futuristic when he talked to the Disciples and even when he gave answer to the High Priest. Even Peter's discourse in the Acts dates his messiahship from the moment of the Resurrection. Until then he was Jesus of Nazareth. Only, the provisional condition of sitting on the right hand of God takes the place of the coming upon the clouds of heaven. "Jesus the Nazarene, a man approved of God unto you by mighty works and wonders and signs which God did by him in the midst of you (Acts 2:22), him did God raise up (Acts 2:32) and hath made him both Lord and Messiah, this Jesus whom ye crucified" (Acts 2:36).

This testimony to the primitive conception of Jesus' messiahship is of itself so weighty that it would put to silence the whole Synoptical tradition if that were of a different tenor. How is it conceivable that the Disciples proclaimed that Jesus had entered upon his messianic existence through the Resurrection, if already upon earth he had spoken of his messiahship as a dignity then actually possessed? As a matter of fact the early Synoptic tradition and the view of the primitive Church agree together completely. Both affirm with one voice that Jesus' messianic consciousness was futuristic.

If we had not this witness, the knowledge of Jesus'

historical character and personality would be forever closed to us. For after his death all sorts of presumptions arose to obscure the consciousness of the futuristic character of his messiahship. His resurrection as Messiah coincided with the general Resurrection which should usher in the messianic age—such was the perspective of the Disciples before his death. After his death his resurrection as Messiah constituted a fact for itself. Jesus was the Messiah *before* the messianic age! That is the fateful shifting of the perspective. Therein lies the tragical element—but the magnificent as well—in the whole phenomenon of Christianity.

The primitive Christian consciousness made the most strenuous efforts to fill the breach, trying in spite of it to conceive of Jesus' resurrection as the dawn of the messianic era in the general rising of the dead. There was an effort to make it intelligible as analogous to a somewhat protracted interval between two scenes of the first act of a drama. Properly, however, they already stood within the messianic Resurrection. Thus for Paul, Jesus Christ, proved to be the Messiah through the Resurrection of the dead, "is the first fruits of them that sleep" (I Cor. 15:20). The whole structure of Pauline theology and ethics rests upon this thought. Because they find themselves within this period, believers are in reality buried with Christ and with him raised again through baptism. They are "new" creatures, they are the "righteous," whose citizenship is in heaven. Until we grasp this fundamental notion we cannot perceive the unity in the manifold complications of St. Paul's world of thought.

The Christian historical tradition sought another way out. It assumed a sort of preresurrection which coincided with the resurrection of Jesus. It lent to this the colouring of the messianic Day. Mt. 27:50–53 furnishes an example in legendary form of such a method of reconciling fact and theory. With Jesus' death upon the cross a new world-era dawned. When he yielded up his spirit the veil of the Temple was rent from the top to the bottom and earthquakes, the signs of the end of the world, shook the earth; the rocks were rent; the graves opened; and many bodies of the saints that had fallen asleep were raised. After Jesus' resurrection they go forth out of the tombs into the holy city and appear unto many. So this narrative clings to the conception that the general Resurrection of the dead under the omens of the messianic Day comes in conjunction with Jesus' death and consequent resurrection,—but still only as a sort of prelude.

Time, indeed, proved mightier than the original conceptions. Inexorably it thrust itself like a splitting wedge between Jesus' resurrection and the expected general Resurrection of the messianic Day, and with the temporal coincidence it destroyed also the casual connection in the original sense. The messiahship of Jesus stood up solidly out of the past. Those who confessed it and at the same time expected the Kingdom as a future event lost all consciousness of the fact that in the preaching of Jesus his messiahship and the Kingdom were both of them future and coincident events. They began to regard the Gospel history from the point of view that *Jesus was the Messiah.* The title for this new view of the Gospel history was written by St. Paul. It reads: *"Jesus Christ,"*—the office and dignity of the risen Lord is combined with the historical personality in one idea. The Fourth Gospel has drawn the logical consequence therefrom and has so depicted the history of Jesus as if he had come upon earth as the Messiah.

It is the task of the historical investigator to emancipate himself for a moment from the unhistorical perspective and place the Synoptic accounts in the right light. Only then, when one has grasped the futuristic element in Jesus' messianic consciousness, can one understand why he revealed his dignity to the Disciples as a "secret," why he designated himself thereby as the Son of Man, and in what sense he spoke of his resurrection.

5. *The Betrayal by Judas—the Last Disclosure of the Secret of Messiahship*

What did Judas actually betray? According to the accounts of our Gospels it looks as if he had informed the Sanhedrin where at a particular hour they could apprehend Jesus. But, even if this indication of the place did play some part in the betrayal of Judas, it could only have been incidental. Where Jesus abode they could at any time find out, since he did nothing to make his coming and going secret. If then they desired to seize him, they had only to send a spy after him as he left Jerusalem in the evening, and they could have got all the information they wanted. For this purpose they did not need one of the inner circle.

As a matter of fact, however, the principal difficulty lay in an entirely different direction. Not to *arrest* him but to *convict* him was what they could not accomplish, for they could bring nothing against him. With respect to him and his following they found themselves in the embarrassing fix into which every conscientious church discipline must necessarily fall some time or another: these people were too pious for them, pious beyond proper limits, inasmuch as they with too great enthusiasm believed what the others with seemly moderation of feeling confessed in their creed,—namely, that the Kingdom is near. They could not get a conviction on the ground of the title of Forerunner which the people attributed to him, for he had justified this attribution by signs. Moreover he had never openly claimed for himself such a dignity. Nevertheless the manner of his behaviour was for them dangerous in the highest degree. At the head of the pious populace he terrorised them. For this reason they would gladly have made away with him—and could not.

One can understand the attitude of the Sanhedrin and their difficulties if one steadily keeps in mind that, in view of Jesus' whole activity, the thought had not occurred to anybody that he could take himself to be the Messiah. Thus they knew no charge to bring against him, and had nothing for it but to try to catch him in his speech and discredit him with the people—and in this they were not successful.

Then Judas appeared before them and put the deadly weapon into their hand. As they heard what he told them "they were glad," for now was he delivered into their power. Judas now seeks a favourable moment to deliver the betrayed into their hands (Mk. 14:11).

What he had betrayed to them we can see from the process of the trial. The witnesses of the Pharisees can adduce nothing that would justify his conviction. When, however, the witnesses have withdrawn, the High Priest puts the question to Jesus directly, whether he is the Messiah. To prove such a claim on Jesus' part they could not adduce the necessary witnesses,—for there were none. The High Priest is here in possession of Jesus' secret. That was the betrayal of Judas! Through him the Sanhedrin knew that Jesus claimed to be something different from what the people held him to be, though he raised no protest against it.

They got the decisive charge through the betrayed secret of Cæsarea Philippi. To be Elijah, the prophet of the last times, was no religious crime. But to claim to be

Messiah, that was blasphemy! The perfidy of the charge lay in the High Priest's insinuation that Jesus held himself then to be the Messiah, just as he stood there before him. This Jesus repudiated with a proud word about his coming as Son of Man. Nevertheless he was condemned for blasphemy.

We have therefore three revelations of the secret of messiahship, which so hang together that each subsequent one implies the foregoing. On the mountain near Bethsaida was revealed to the Three the secret which was disclosed to Jesus at his baptism. That was after the harvest. A few weeks later it was known to the Twelve, by the fact that Peter at Cæsarea Philippi answered Jesus' question out of the knowledge which he had attained upon the mountain. One of the Twelve betrayed the secret to the High Priest. This last revelation of the secret was fatal, for it brought about the death of Jesus. *He was condemned as Messiah although he had never appeared in that rôle.*

CHAPTER IX

The Secret of the Passion

1. *The Pre-Messianic Affliction*

The reference to the Passion belonged as a matter of course to the eschatological prediction. A time of unheard of affliction must precede the coming of the Kingdom. Out of these woes the Messiah will be brought to birth. That was a view prevalent far and wide: in no other wise could the events of the last times be imagined.

According to this view Jesus' words must be interpreted. It will appear then that in his preaching of the Kingdom he brought into sharp prominence the thought of the Affliction of the last times. We always assume that when he speaks of persecutions which his Disciples shall encounter he means to predict what they must go through when they are left alone and orphaned on earth after his death. That is totally false. After his death Jesus will be Messiah through the Resurrection, and therewith the glory of the Kingdom dawns. Not what they must withstand after his death, but what they are to be in the Kingdom is the thought which concerns the Disciples on the way to Jerusalem.

When Jesus speaks of suffering and persecution it is a question of the afflictions which his followers must bear with him before the dawn of the Kingdom. What is meant is the last desperate attack of the powers of this world at enmity with God, which shall sweep like a flood over those who in expectation of the Kingdom represent the divine power in the godless world. Hence Jesus constitutes the focus upon which the Affliction concentrates. He is the rock upon which the waves dash themselves to pieces. Whosoever would not be torn away by the flood must cling stedfastly to him.

When he says that his mission is not to bring peace upon earth but a sword, when he speaks of the uprising which he brings about, in which the most sacred earthly ties shall be broken, in which one must follow him laden with the cross and count one's earthly life for naught (Mt. 10:34–42), he means by this the great persecution of the last times. He who hastens the coming of the Kingdom brings also this Affliction to pass, for it is out of this travail indeed that the Kingdom and the Messiah are born.

Hence the harsh accord heard throughout the messianic harmonies! Jesus concludes the Beatitudes with the intimation that his Disciples are blessed if they are hated and persecuted and all manner of evil is spoken against them for his sake. Then have they indeed reason to rejoice and be exceeding glad, for in what they must endure is revealed their right to membership in the Kingdom of God. While they are still afflicted by the power of this world their reward is already prepared in heaven (Mt. 5:11, 12).

"Preach, saying, the Kingdom of God is at hand," was Jesus' injunction to the Apostles when sending them out. Therewith, however, he prepared them impressively for the Affliction of the last times, for the hand of the world-clock approaches the great hour. They must know it, in order that they may not think that something strange has befallen them when they are brought to trial by the world-power, when uprising and persecution threaten them and bring their life into danger. They must know it, in order that they may not doubt and deny him and be offended in him when he is delivered into the hands of men, for he himself as the mighty preacher of the Kingdom has incited this uprising. When, however, the world-power appears to conquer, then God in his omnipotence stands above. Not those that kill the body must they fear, but the almighty Lord who in the Judgment can destroy both soul and body in hell. In this last uprising the world-power judges itself: after the Judgment comes the Kingdom. That is the fundamental thought of the charge to the Apostles.

Likewise the embassage to the Baptist concludes with a similar intimation. The Kingdom is near, he would have them say to him; my preaching, signs, and wonders confirm it; and he attains blessedness whosoever is not offended in me, i.e. whosoever is faithful to me in the premessianic Affliction.

His warning of the heavy time to come is directed most impressively, however, to those whom the Apostles' preaching has drawn about him in trustful expectation of the Kingdom. In the gathering dusk of evening he had celebrated with them the great Supper beside the sea. As one who knew himself to be the Messiah he had distributed to them sacred food, and thereby, without their suspecting it, had consecrated them to be partakers of the messianic feast. The following morning, however, he called them about him at Bethsaida and exhorted them to be ready to sacrifice their life in the Affliction. Whosoever shall be ashamed of him and of his words in the humiliation which must overtake him in this adulterous and sinful world, him will the Son of Man refuse to recognise when he shall appear in the glory of his Father surrounded by his angels (Mk. 8:35–38).

2. *The Idea of the Passion in the First Period*

The Passion therefore belonged to Jesus' preaching

from the beginning. In the Affliction of the last times his followers must pass with him through suffering to glory—so his hearers understood him. Only, they did not know that he with whom they must suffer would be revealed as Messiah.

In Jesus' messianic consciousness the thought of suffering acquired now, as applied to himself, a mysterious significance. The messiahship which he became aware of at his baptism was not a possession, nor a mere object of expectation; but in the eschatological conception it was implied as a matter of course that through the trial of suffering he must become what God had destined him to be. His messianic consciousness was never without the thought of the Passion. Suffering is the way to the revelation of messiahship!

What he experienced in this age represented the hidden life and labour of the Messiah. Suffering, however, was allotted to this rôle. It was Jewish doctrine that the Messiah must be full of chastisement, for the sufferings are necessary to the making of the perfectly righteous man.[1]

This messianic consciousness of Jesus shows the same deepening of moral tone as does his eschatology. According to the customary modernising conception, it is assumed that during the greater part of his ministry Jesus did not think of the Passion, but was first obliged to entertain that thought by the malicious enmity of the Scribes. Thus his messiahship receives in the first period an ethical-idyllic cast, in the second, a modern hue of resignation. The historic-eschatological picture is at once livelier, deeper, and more moral. Jesus' character did not undergo an "evolution" through the acceptance of the idea of the Passion. From the beginning he knew himself as Messiah only in so far as he was resolved through suffering to be

[1] Weber, p. 343.

purified unto perfection. As the one who is destined to bear rule in the new age he must beforehand be delivered into the power of ungodliness in order that he may there approve himself for the divine lordship he is to exercise. Out of such a messianic consciousness as this he adjures those about him to remain true so that he can recognise them as his own when the glory dawns. Thus the active ethical trait which constituted the depth of the secret of the Kingdom is a controlling factor also in the secret of messiahship.

The historical problem presents itself now in this form: In the first period Jesus expressed the thought of the Passion much more frequently than in the second, and he uttered it openly. Every discourse of some length concludes with such an intimation. His own Disciples were familiar with the thought of seeing him humiliated in the Affliction. In spite of this, however, the disclosure at Cæsarea Philippi appeared to the Disciples a new thing, and so it was in fact. For it was no longer a question simply of the suffering which the great herald of the Kingdom must undergo in company with his own in the final Affliction; but now he suffers who is to be the Messiah. This suffering, moreover, does not any longer occur in the general Affliction of the last times, but Jesus suffers alone, and his suffering is now represented as a purely earthly, historical event! He will be delivered to the Council and by it condemned to death! That was the new thing which remained a secret for the Disciples.

3. *The "Temptation" and the Divine Omnipotence*

A peculiar note of hesitancy appears in the thought of the Passion. At one time death seems an absolute necessity; then again—for example, in Gethsemane—Jesus recognises once more the possibility that the Passion may still be spared him. But as a matter of fact the idea of the Passion subsisted without respect to earthly success or failure. Therefore the hesitancy ought not to be brought into connection with this. As Jesus journeyed towards Jerusalem to die he did not in a corner of his heart indulge the thought that God in his omnipotence might perhaps be able nevertheless to make his way a triumphal march and show himself through him victorious over the Pharisees and the Council. That, according to his feeling, would have been a "human" way of thinking, such as he had reproved in Peter (Mk. 8:33). For in the affairs of God's Kingdom he cannot oppose to one another the opposition of the Scribes and the divine omnipotence; it is a question of a divine drama in which they were mere subordinate actors with a prescribed rôle, like the minions that arrested him at their behest. The hesitancy must therefore have its ground in the divine will itself.

It is the specific characteristic of Jesus' view, that the divine will has indeed, on the one hand, designedly preordained the messianic drama in the well known form; yet, on the other hand again, God remains sovereignly free with respect to his plan. By a messianic programme established once and for all the divine omnipotence behind it is in no wise bound! It knows no determinism at all.

Jesus expected of this omnipotence that it could still receive into the estate of blessedness even such as by their behaviour had forfeited membership in the Kingdom. According to the accepted standards it is indeed impossible that the rich can enter into life. But with God all things are possible (Mk. 10:27).

It was a maxim that whosoever would reign with the coming Messiah must suffer with Jesus. But yet he dared not promise his two intimate Disciples, James and John, the seats upon the throne, although he expected that they would share his Passion. He might by this infringe upon God's omnipotence (Mk. 10:35–40).

Thus the Affliction also of the last times had its place indeed in the divinely ordained course of the messianic drama. But yet it lay in God's unrestricted omnipotence that he might eliminate it and permit the Kingdom to dawn without this season of trial. Therefore men might pray God that he would suffer that heavy hour of probation to pass by. Jesus enjoined this upon his Disciples in the same prayer in which he taught them to make petition for the coming Kingdom. He teaches them to implore God for the final state of blessedness, in which his name will be hallowed and his will be done on earth as it is in heaven; but at the same time they are to beg him not to lead them into the "Temptation," not to give them into the power of the Evil, not to oblige them to make satisfaction for their sins by the endurance of the Affliction of the last times; but to deliver them by his omnipotence from the power of the Evil when the ungodly world for the last time asserts itself at the coming of the Kingdom for which they pray. That is the inner connection of the last three petitions of the Lord's Prayer.

The Lord's Prayer thus exhibits in the first three and the last three petitions a purely eschatological character. We have the same contrast as in the Beatitudes, the charge to the Apostles, the embassage to the Baptist, and the discourse at Bethsaida. First it is a question of the coming of the Kingdom, then of the Affliction of the last times. We perceive from the Lord's Prayer, however, that there is no absolute necessity for this Affliction, but that it is only relatively determined in God's almighty will.

The Affliction, in fact, represents in its extremest form the repentance requisite for the Kingdom. Whosoever comes through that test approved makes satisfaction for his transgressions in the godless æon. Through conflict and suffering men wrest themselves free from this power to become instruments of the divine will in the Kingdom of God. That is to be conceived collectively. The faithful adherents of the Kingdom as a community make the satisfaction. The individual thereby perfects and approves himself. Such is God's will. Jesus, however, prays with them to God that he may be pleased in his omnipotence to forgive them the debt without satisfaction, as they forgive their debtors. That means remission pure and simple, without atonement. May it please God not to lead them through the "Temptation," but straightway to release them from the power of the world.

Only so can one understand how Jesus throughout his ministry can assume forgiveness of sins and yet here expressly prays for it; and how he can speak of a temptation which comes from God. It is a question in fact of the general messianic remission of debts and the Temptation of the messianic Affliction. Therefore these petitions constitute the conclusion of the Kingdom-prayer.

What Jesus here in common prayer petitions for the community, that he implores for himself when his hour is come. In Gethsemane he prostrates himself before God. In moving prayer he appeals to God's omnipotence: Abba, Father, all things are possible unto thee (Mk. 14:36). He would that the cup of suffering might pass his lips without his needing to taste it. Also he rouses the three Disciples, bidding them to watch and pray God that he may spare them the Temptation, for the flesh is weak.

4. *The Idea of the Passion in the Second Period*

With the revelation at Cæsarea Philippi cease all intimations that the believers must pass with Jesus through the Affliction. According to the secret which he imparts to the Disciples he alone suffers. In Jerusalem he addressed not one urgent word, either to the people or to the Disciples, about following him in suffering. Indeed he actually takes back what he before had said. The morning after the Supper by the seashore, addressing those whom he had consecrated unto the messianic banquet, he makes their blessedness dependent upon following him in suffering. To the partakers of the Last Supper at Jerusalem he calmly stated beforehand that they would all be "offended" in him that night! He coupled this with no condemnation—for it is so determined in the Scripture! Is it not written, "I will smite the shepherd, and the sheep shall be scattered"? Therefore, even if they are offended in him, if even they forsake him, in his glory he will still gather them again, and as Messiah—for that he is as the risen one—he will go before them unto Galilee (Mk. 14:26, 28).

What at an earlier period he had required of all, that he now does not expect even of him who boasted that he alone would stand by him. "Before the cock crow twice thou shalt deny me thrice," said he to Peter (Mk. 14:29, 31).

This change must be connected with the form which the idea of the Passion assumed in the second period. There must have occurred an alteration in the conception of the Affliction of the last times. The others are freed from the trial of suffering, Jesus suffers alone;—and in fact the humiliation consists in the death to which the scribes consign him. It is by this means that the final affliction now accomplishes itself. His faithful followers are spared. *He suffers in their stead, for he gives his life a ransom for many.*

Jesus has not disclosed in what way this secret was

made known to him in the days of solitude after the mission of the Twelve. The form of the secret of the Passion shows, however, that two experiences had influence upon him.

First, the death of the Baptist. The Baptist for him was Elijah. If he was slain by the hand of man before the messianic Day, such was God's will, and so it was foreordained in the messianic drama. This occurred while the Disciples were away. His embassage to the Baptist perhaps never reached him. He must come now to an understanding of this matter. For this cause he wishes to withdraw into solitude with his companions.

How much he was preoccupied with the thought of the Baptist's death is shown by the conversation which followed the revelation to the Three on the mountain. It was ordained in the Scripture that Elijah must meet such a fate at the hands of men. So also it is written of the Son of Man that he must suffer many things and be set at naught (Mk. 9:12, 13).

Hitherto he had spoken only in general terms of the final Affliction as an event of the last times. Now, however, it has been fulfilled upon the Baptist as an *historical event*. That is a sign, which indicates how it will be fulfilled upon himself.

This indication came precisely at the time when he was compelled by the course of events to reflect upon the final Affliction. After the return of the Twelve he had expected it as an impending event. But it failed to occur. What is more, the Kingdom failed therewith to appear! In sending out the Twelve he had told them that they would be surprised by the overflowing woes ere they had gone through all the cities of Israel,—and they had returned without witnessing the beginning of the woes or the dawn of the Kingdom.

The report with which they returned showed, however, that all was ready. Already the power of ungodliness was broken, for else the unclean spirits would not have been subject to them. The Kingdom was compellingly hastened by the repentance practised since the days of the Baptist. In this respect also the measure was full,—that was proved by the multitudes which thronged about him in faithful expectation. So all was ready—and still the Kingdom did not come! The delay of the eschatological coming of the Kingdom,—that was the great fact which drove Jesus at that time once and again into solitude to seek light upon the mystery.

Before the Kingdom could come the Affliction must arrive. But it failed to arrive. It must be brought about in order that the Kingdom may thus be constrained to come. Repentance and the subjugation of the power of ungodliness did not avail by themselves; but the violent stormers of the Kingdom must be reinforced by one stronger still, the future Messiah, who brings down upon himself the final Affliction in the form in which it had already been accomplished upon Elijah. Thus the secret of the Kingdom merges in the secret of the Passion.

The conception of the final Affliction contains the thought of atonement and purification. All they who are destined for the Kingdom must win forgiveness for the guilt contracted in the earthly æon by encountering stedfastly the world-power as it collects itself for a last attack. For through this guilt they were still subject to the power of ungodliness. This guilt constitutes a counter weight which holds back the coming of the Kingdom.

But now God does not bring the Affliction to pass. And yet the atonement must be made. Then it occurred to Jesus that he as the coming Son of Man must accomplish the atonement in his own person. He who one day shall reign over the believers as Messiah now humbles himself under them and serves them by giving his life a ransom for many, in order that the Kingdom may dawn upon them. That is his mission in the estate which precedes his celestial glory. "For this he is come" (Mk. 10:45). He must suffer for the sins of those who are ordained for his Kingdom. In order to carry this out, he journeys up to Jerusalem, that there he may be put to death by the secular authority, just as Elijah who went before him suffered at the hand of Herod. That is the secret of the Passion. Jesus did actually die for the sins of men, even though it was in another sense than that which Anselm's theory assumes.

5. *Isaiah 40:66: The Secret of the Passion Foretold in the Scripture*

"How is it written of the Son of Man? That he must suffer many things and be set at naught" (Mk. 9:12). The new form of the secret of the Passion is derived from the Scripture. In the picture of the suffering servant of God Jesus recognised himself. There he found his vocation of suffering depicted in advance.

In order, however, to understand how his secret came to him from out the Scripture, the picture of the suffering servant of God must be set in the great framework in which it belongs. The modern-historical solution cannot do this. It confines itself to the notion of a meek self-surrender. As soon, however, as it is once perceived that Jesus' idea of the Passion was eschatological, it is evident also in what a great context he must view the figure of the suffering servant of God. Accordingly, Isaiah 40:66 was nothing else but the prophetic representation of the events of the last time in the midst of which he knew himself to be.

The passage commences with the proclamation that God's reign is about to begin. The preparer of the way comes upon the scene. He cries that the earthly passes away when the Lord, dealing reward and recompense, appears in his glory. The hour dawns in which he gathers his flock and brings in the era of peace.

The Elect is there. He proclaims righteousness in truth. God has put his spirit upon him (Isai. 42:1 ff). He shall establish judgment upon the earth; the cities wait upon his teaching. But before the glory dawns and the bearer of the divine spirit rules with power and righteousness over the peoples he must pass through an estate of humiliation. Others do not understand why he is put to shame. They think God has rejected him, and know not that he bears their infirmities, is pierced for their transgressions, and smitten for their offences. The oppressed servant is meek and openeth not his mouth. For the transgression of the people he is stricken to death. Then, however, will the Lord glorify him. He hath called him to this from his mother's womb. He is ordained to bring again Jacob and to save Israel. He shall be for a light to the Gentiles, that God's salvation may extend unto the ends of the earth (Isai. 49:1 ff; 52:1 ff; 53:1 ff).

Upon the delineation of the suffering of the servant of God there follows a description of the judgment upon the whole world and upon Israel (Isai. 54–65). In the end, however, the glory of God breaks forth. He is enthroned above the new heaven and the new earth (Isai. 65–66). When the Judgment is accomplished, then the rejoicing breaks out, for the blessed out of the whole world, out of every tribe and nation, will gather unto him and do him reverence.

One must grasp the dramatic unity in these chapters in order to enter into sympathy with one who sought here mysterious intimation about the things of the last time.

Jesus' idea of the Passion is in the end completely absorbed in that of the Deutero-Isaiah. Like the servant of God, he too is destined to reign in glory. But first he appears, meek and unrecognised, in the rôle of a preacher who works righteousness. He must pass also through suffering and humiliation ere God permit the glorious consummation to dawn. What he endures is an atonement for the iniquity of others. This is a secret between himself and God. The others cannot and need not understand it, for when the glory dawns they will recognise that he has suffered for them. Wherefore Jesus did not need to explain his Passion to the people and to the Disciples, and ought not to do so. It must remain a secret,—so it is written in the Scripture. Even to those to whom he foretold what was coming he uttered it as a secret. At his appearing as Son of Man the scales must fall from their eyes. In the glory of the Kingdom they then shall recognise that he has suffered in order that they may be spared and have peace. The secret is intelligible only retrospectively, from the point of view of the glory that shall be revealed.

Therefore it makes no difference if his own followers turn away from him in his humiliation and men are offended in him as though he were chastised of God. The Scripture does not reckon it against them as sacrilege, but has so ordained it. The moment therefore the secret of the Passion is made clear to him by the Scripture he no more says, Whosoever is ashamed of me in my humiliation, the same is condemned; but, Ye shall all be offended in me,—knowing at the same time that they all shall be gathered about him at the Resurrection.

Under the influence, therefore, of the Deutero-Isaiah the idea of the general Affliction of the last times was transformed into the personal secret of Jesus' Passion.

6. *The "Human" Element in the Secret of the Passion*

The innermost nature of the idea of suffering underwent no change in consequence of the secret of the Passion of the second epoch. For Jesus, suffering, even in this form, remained pre-eminently the moral condition of the dignity ordained to him.

Now, however, the Affliction exhibits the concrete traits of a determinate event. Jesus brings it down from the vague heights of apocalyptic drama to the level of human history. Therein lies something prophetic of the future of Christianity. After Jesus' death the whole messianic drama of the last times is dissolved in human history. This development began with the secret of the Passion.

Thus it is, too, that the secret of the Passion, as compared with the idea of suffering of the first period, exhibits more human traits. There is a quality of compassionate consideration for others in the thought that he makes satisfaction in the Passion for the adherents of the Kingdom, in order that they may be exempted from the trial in which perchance they might prove weak. The petition, "Lead us not into the Temptation, but deliver us from the Evil," is now fulfilled in his Passion.

This deeply human trait is especially evident in Gethsemane. Only over the three intimate Disciples still hovers the possibility that they may be obliged to pass with him through suffering and temptation. The sons of Zebedee, to secure their claim to sit with him upon the throne, boasted that they could drink with him his cup and undergo with him the baptism of suffering—and this prospect he held out to them (Mk. 10:38, 40). Peter, however, swore that he would not deny him; even if all others should forsake him, he desired to die with him (Mk. 14:31). These three Jesus had taken with him to the place where he prayed. While he implored God that the cup might pass him by, there overcame him a sorrowful anxiety for the Three. If God does now actually send them with him through the Passion, will they hold out as they are bold to believe? Wherefore he is mindful of them in that sad hour. Twice he arouses himself and wakes them out of sleep, bidding them watch and pray to God that he lead them not into the Temptation, even if he will not spare him this cup; for the spirit is willing, but the flesh is weak. That is perhaps the most touching moment in Jesus' life. Some have dared to call Gethsemane Jesus' weak hour; but in reality it is precisely the hour in which his supernatural greatness is revealed in his deeply human compassion.

7. *The Idea of the Passion in the Primitive Church. The Shifting of the Perspective*

Jesus carried with him to the grave the secret of the Passion which was to be revealed to the inheritors of the Kingdom at its coming. But the Kingdom did not come. Thus it is to be explained that though he indeed had given intimation of his Passion to the Disciples, yet they, when the event came to pass, knew no interpretation of it. Nevertheless, in some way they had to explain it, by the help of such intimations as they could recall. This accounts for the fact that the theory of the early Church regarding the Passion of Jesus was far poorer than his Secret. The explanation of the Church focussed principally upon one fact: In consequence of the Passion and the Resurrection from the dead he is the Messiah. In this sense the Passion and the Exaltation are foreordained in the Scripture.

While Jesus' secret brought his death and the dawning of the Kingdom into the closest temporal and causal connection, for the primitive Church, on the other hand, a past event, as such, constituted the object to be explained, since the Kingdom had not arrived and the original causal connection was dissolved along with the temporal.

Now with reference to his death Jesus had spoken also of atonement and forgiveness of sins. But the thoughts which he associated therewith, the events had rendered entirely impossible. The indefinite "many," who were to apply the ransom to themselves in the knowledge that he had suffered for them, simply did not exist; for the Kingdom had not yet appeared. Only from that point of vantage, however, could one apprehend that he had performed the Atonement of Affliction for the inheritors of the Kingdom.

In the meantime the situation was entirely different: "the believers" had taken the place of the "many." Those who believe in the messiahship of Jesus have the forgiveness of sins,—this sentence, as the sermon at Pentecost shows, was a constituent of the earlier Apostolic preaching (Acts 2:38). But to what extent one had thereby forgiveness of sins,—in that consisted the problem. This, however, was historically insoluble, for according to Jesus' secret of the Passion the forgiveness of sins applied not to those who believe in Jesus-Christ, but to the inheritors of the Kingdom. Therefore, however profound they may be, and however true to the religious consciousness of their time, none of the attempts to explain the significance of the Passion, from Paul to Ritschl, apprehend the thought of Jesus, because they proceed upon an entirely different assumption.

As all of these theories sought nevertheless to legitimate themselves historically, we witness the astonishing spectacle, that the most diverse interpretations of his Passion are put into the mouth of Jesus,—of which, however, not one can even remotely explain how out of such a conception the primitive Apostolic estimate of the Death could have been derived. The same is true of the modern-historical solution. If Jesus taught the Disciples to understand the ethical significance of his death, why did the primitive Christian explanation of the Passion confine itself to the notion of conformity with Scripture and the "forgiveness of sins"?

To this question the modern-historical solution furnishes no answer. The eschatologico-historical, on the other hand, is able to take account perspectively of the necessary distortion which Jesus' idea of the Passion underwent in the primitive Church. It indicates which elements alone of the Passion secret could still subsist after his death. Because it grasps the connection between the early Christian interpretation and the thought of Jesus the eschatologico-historical solution is the right one.

The abolition of the causal connection between the death of Jesus and the realisation of the Kingdom was fatal to the early Christian eschatology. With the secret of the Passion, the secret of the Kingdom likewise perished. This, however, meant nothing less than that eschatology lost precisely that specific "Christian" character which Jesus had imparted to it. The active ethical element which served to moralise it dropped out. Thus the eschatology of the early Church was "dechristianised" by Jesus' death. Therewith it sank back again to the level of contemporary Jewish thought. The Kingdom is again an object of expectation merely. That moral conversion is effective actively to hasten its coming,—this secret was buried with Jesus. Now men repented and strove after moral renewal *as in the days of the Baptist.*

This dechristianising was manifest especially in the matter of the final Affliction. According to the Passion idea of the first period, the believers must suffer along with the Messiah; according to that of the second, he was resolved to endure the Affliction for them. In the early Church the believers expected the Affliction *before* the appearing of the Messiah, as was the case in the contemporary Jewish conception; for the Passion secret of Jesus was not known to them. Therefore the Jewish apocalypses belonged to them just as much as to the other Jews, only with the difference that the crucified Jesus was to be the coming Messiah. Early Christian eschatology was therefore still "Christian" only through the *person* of Jesus, no longer through his *spirit,* as was the case in the secret of the Kingdom of God and in the secret of the Passion.

This furnishes a criterion for judging "the Synoptic apocalypse" (Mk. 13). Even though it may contain single eschatological sayings attributable to Jesus, the discourse as such is necessarily unhistorical. It betrays the perspective of the time after Jesus' death. During the days at Jerusalem Jesus could speak of no general Affliction before the coming of the Son of Man. The Synoptic apocalypse stands in direct contradiction to the secret of the Passion, since this indeed simply abolishes the general Affliction of the last times. Therefore it is unhistorical. Apocalyptic discourses with intimation of the final Affliction belong to the Galilean period at the time of the mission of the Twelve. The discourse to the Apostles on that occasion is the historical Synoptic apocalypse. About a time of affliction after his death Jesus never uttered a word to his Disciples, for it lay beyond his field of vision.

Therefore with the death of Jesus, and precisely by reason of it, eschatology—notwithstanding that the primitive Christian community still completely lived in it—was virtually done away with. It was destined to be forced out of the Christian *Weltanschauung,* for it was "dechristianised" by the fact that in parting with the secret of the Kingdom of God and the idea of the Passion it had forfeited also the inner ethical life which was breathed into it by Jesus. A tree in full bloom stricken at the root, —such was the fate of eschatology, to wilt and wither, although no one at first suspected it was doomed. In the fact that subsequent history compulsorily created in the Church an uneschatological view of the world, it only accomplished what in the nature of things was already determined by Jesus' death.

The death of Jesus the end of eschatology! The Messiah who upon earth was not such—the end of the messianic expectation! The view of the world in which Jesus lived and preached was eschatological: the "Christian view of the world" which he founded by his death carries mankind forever beyond eschatology! That is the great secret of the Christian "scheme of salvation."

For Jesus and his Disciples his death was, according to the eschatological view, merely a *transitional* event. As soon, however, as the event occurred it became the *central fact* upon which the new, uneschatological view was built up. In primitive Christianity the old and new were still side by side.

The adherents of Jesus believed in the coming of the Kingdom because his imposing personality accredited the message. The Church after his death believed in his messiahship and expected the coming of the Kingdom. We believe that in his ethical-religious personality, as revealed in his ministry and suffering, the Messiah and the Kingdom are come.

The situation may be likened to the course of the sun. Its brightness breaks forth while it is still behind the mountains. The dark clouds take colour from its rays, and the conflict of light and darkness produces a play of fantastic imagery. The sun itself is not yet visible: it is there only in the sense that the light issues from it. As the sun behind the morning glow,—so appeared the personality of Jesus of Nazareth to his contemporaries in the pre-messianic age.

At the moment when the heaven glows with intensest colouring the sun itself rises above the horizon. But with this the wealth of colour begins gradually to diminish. The fantastic images pale and vanish because the sun itself dissolves the clouds upon which they are formed. As the rising sun above the horizon,—so appeared Jesus Christ to the primitive Church in its eschatological expectation.

As the sun at midday,—so he appears to us. We know nothing of morning and evening glow; we see only the white brilliance which pervades all. But the fact that the sun now shines for us in such a light does not justify us in conceiving the sunrise also as if it were a brilliant disk of midday brightness emerging above the horizon. Our modern view of Jesus' death is true, true in its inmost nature, because it reflects his ethical-religious personality in the thoughts of our time. But when we import this into the history of Jesus and of primitive Christianity we commit the same blunder as were we to paint the sunrise without the morning glow.

In genuine historical knowledge there is liberating and helping power. Our faith is built upon the personality of Jesus. But between our world-view and that in which he lived and laboured there lies a deep and seemingly unbridgeable gulf. Men therefore saw themselves obliged to detach as it were his personality from his world-view and touch it up with modern colours.

This produced a picture of Jesus which was strangely lifeless and vague. One got a hybrid figure, half modern, half antique. With much else that is modern, men transferred to him our modern psychology, without always recognising clearly that it is not applicable to him and necessarily belittles him. For it is derived from mediocre minds which are a patchwork of opinions and apprehend and observe themselves only in a constant flux of development. Jesus, however, is a superhuman personality moulded in one piece.

Thus modern theology does violence to history and psychology, inasmuch as it cannot prove what right we have to segregate Jesus from his age, to translate his personality into the terms of our modern thought, and to conceive of him as "Messiah" and "Son of God" outside of the Jewish framework.

Genuine historical knowledge, however, restores to theology full freedom of movement! It presents to it the personality of Jesus in an eschatological world-view, yet one which is modern through and through because *His* mighty spirit pervades it.

This Jesus is far greater than the one conceived in modern terms: he is really a superhuman personality. With his death he destroyed the form of his *Weltanschauung,* rendering his own eschatology impossible. Thereby he gives to all peoples and to all times the right to apprehend him in terms of their thoughts and conceptions, in order that his spirit may pervade their "Weltanschauung" as it quickened and transfigured the Jewish eschatology.

Therefore may modern theology, just by reason of a genuine historical knowledge, claim freedom of movement, without being hampered continually by petty historical expedients which nowadays are often resorted to at the expense of historical veracity. Theology is not bound to graze in a paddock. It is free, for its task is to found our Christian view of the world solely upon the personality of Jesus Christ, irrespective of the form in which it expressed itself in his time. He himself has destroyed this form with his death. History prompts theology to this unhistorical step.

As Jesus gave up the ghost, the Roman centurion said, "Truly this man was the Son of God" (Mk. 15:39). Thus at the moment of his death the lofty dignity of Jesus was set free for expression in all tongues, among all nations, and for all philosophies.

CHAPTER X

Summary of the Life of Jesus

The "Life of Jesus" is limited to the last months of his existence on earth. At the season of the summer seed-sowing he began his ministry and ended it upon the cross at Easter of the following year.

His public ministry may be counted in weeks. The first period extends from seed time to harvest; the second comprises the days of his appearance in Jerusalem. Autumn and winter he spent in heathen territory alone with his Disciples.

Before him the Baptist had appeared and had borne emphatic witness to the nearness of the Kingdom and the coming of the mighty pre-messianic Forerunner, with whose appearance the pouring out of the Holy Ghost should take place. According to Joel, this among other miracles was the sign that the Day of Judgment was imminent. John himself never imagined that he was this Forerunner; nor did such a thought occur to the people, for he had not ushered in the age of miracles. He is a prophet,—that was the universal opinion.

About Jesus' earlier development we know nothing. All lies in the dark. Only this is sure: at his baptism the secret of his existence was disclosed to him,—namely, that he was the one whom God had destined to be the Messiah. With this revelation he was complete, and underwent no further development. For now he is assured that, until the near coming of the messianic age which was to reveal his glorious dignity, he has to labour for the Kingdom as the unrecognised and hidden Messiah, and must approve and purify himself together with his friends in the final Affliction.

The idea of suffering was thus included in his messianic consciousness, just as the notion of the pre-messianic Affliction was indissolubly connected with the expectation of the Kingdom. Earthly events could not influence Jesus' course. His secret raised him above the world, even though he still walked as a man among men.

His appearing and his proclamation have to do only with the near approach of the Kingdom. His preaching is that of John, only that he confirms it by signs. Although his secret controls all his preaching, yet no one may know of it, for he must remain unrecognised till the new æon dawns.

Like his secret, so also is his whole ethical outlook ruled by the contrast of "Now and Then." It is a question of repentance unto the Kingdom, and the conquest of the righteousness which renders one fit for it,—for only the righteous inherit the Kingdom. This righteousness is higher than that of the Law, for he knows that the law and the Prophets prophesied until John,—with the Baptist, however, one finds oneself in the age of the Forerunner, immediately before the dawn of the Kingdom.

Therefore, as the future Messiah, he must preach and work that higher morality. The poor in spirit, the meek, those that endure suffering, those that hunger and thirst after righteousness, the merciful, the pure in heart, the peacemakers,—these all are blessed because by this mark they are destined for the Kingdom.

Behind this ethical preaching looms the secret of the Kingdom of God. That which, as performed by the individual, constitutes moral renewal in preparation for the Kingdom, signifies, as accomplished by the community, a fact through which the realisation of the Kingdom in a supernatural way will be hastened. Thus individual and social ethics blend in the great secret. As the plentiful harvest, by God's wonderful working, follows mysteriously upon the sowing, so comes also the Kingdom of God, by reason of man's moral renewal, but substantially without his assistance.

The parable contains also the suggestion of a chronological coincidence. Jesus spoke at the season of seed-sowing and expected the Kingdom at the time of the harvest. Nature was God's clock. With the last seed-sowing he had set it for the last time.

The secret of the Kingdom of God is the transfiguration in celestial light of the ethics of the early prophets, according to which also the final state of glory will be brought about by God only on condition of the moral conversion of Israel. In sovereign style Jesus effects the synthesis of the apocalyptic of Daniel and the ethics of the Prophets. With him it is not a question of eschatological ethics, rather is his world view an ethical eschatology. As such it is modern.

The signs and wonders also come under a double point of view. For the people they are merely to confirm the preaching of the nearness of the Kingdom. Whosoever now does not believe that the time is so far advanced, he has no excuse. The signs and wonders condemn him, for they plainly attest that the power of ungodliness is coming to an end.

For Jesus, however, there lay behind this affirmation the secret of the Kingdom of God. When the Pharisees wished to ascribe these very signs to the power of Satan, he alluded to the secret by a parable. By his acts he binds the power of ungodliness, as one falls upon a strong man and renders him harmless before attempting to rob him of his possessions. Wherefore, in sending out his Apostles, he gives them, together with the charge to preach, authority over unclean spirits. They are to deal the last blow.

A third element in the preaching of the Kingdom was the intimation of the pre-messianic Affliction. The believers must be prepared to pass with him through that time of trial, in which they are to prove themselves the elect of the Kingdom by stedfast resistance to the last attack of the power of the world. This attack will concentrate about his person: therefore they must stand by him even unto death. Only life in God's Kingdom is real life. The Son of Man will judge them according as they have stood by him, Jesus, or no. Thus Jesus at the conclusion of the Beatitudes turns to his own Disciples with the words: "Blessed are ye when men persecute you for my sake." The charge to the Apostles turns into a consideration of the Affliction. The embassage to the Baptist about the imminence of the Kingdom concludes with the word: "Blessed is he whosoever shall not be offended in me." At Bethsaida, the morning after he had celebrated the Supper by the seashore, he adjured the multitude to stand by him, even when he shall become an object of shame and scorn in this sinful world,—their blessedness depends upon this.

This Affliction meant not only a probation but also an atonement. It is foreordained in the messianic drama, because God requires of the adherents of the Kingdom a satisfaction for their transgressions in this æon. But he is almighty. In this omnipotence he determines the question of membership in the Kingdom and the place each shall occupy therein, without himself being bound by any determining cause whatsoever. So also in view of his omnipotence the necessity of the final Affliction is only relative.

He can abrogate it. The last three petitions of the Lord's Prayer contemplate this possibility. After beseeching God that he would send the Kingdom, that his name might be blessed and his will be done on earth as it is in heaven, men beg him to forgive them the transgressions and spare them the Temptation, rescuing them directly from the power of evil.

This was the content of Jesus' preaching during the first period. He remained throughout this time on the northern shore of the lake. Chorazin, Bethsaida, and Capernaum were the principal centres of his activity. From thence he made an excursion across the lake to the region of the Ten Cities and a journey to Nazareth.

Precisely in the towns which were the scenes of his chief activity he encountered unbelief. The curse which he must utter over them is proof of it. The Pharisees, moreover, were hostile and sought to discredit him with the people, on account of his very miracles. In Nazareth he had experience of the fact that a prophet is without honour in his own country.

Thus the Galilean period was anything but a fortunate one. Such outward ill success, however, signified nothing for the coming of the Kingdom. The unbelieving cities merely brought down judgment upon themselves. Jesus had other mysterious indications for measuring the approach of the Kingdom. By these he recognised that the time was come. For this reason he sent forth the Apostles just as they were returning from Nazareth, *for it was harvest time.*

By means of their preaching and their signs the reputation of his mighty personality spread far and wide. Now begins the time of success! John in prison hears of it and sends his disciples to ask him if he is "he that should come," for from his miracles he concluded that the time of the mighty Forerunner whom he had heralded had arrived.

Jesus performed signs, his Disciples had power over the spirits. When he spoke of the Judgment he laid stress upon the fact that the Son of Man stood in such solidarity with him that he would recognise only such as had stood by him, Jesus. The people therefore opined that he might be the one for whom all were looking, and the Baptist desired to have assurance on this point.

Jesus cannot tell him who he is. "The time is far advanced"—that is the gist of his reply. After the departure of the messengers Jesus turned to the people and signified in mysterious terms that the time is indeed much further advanced than the Baptist dreamed in asking such a question. The era of the Forerunner had already begun with the appearance of the Baptist himself. From that time on the Kingdom of God is with violence compelled to draw near. He himself who asks the question is Elijah—if they could comprehend it. Men were not able to perceive that the man in prison was Elijah. When he began his preaching, they knew not the time. That was due not alone to the fact that John performed no miracles, but to the hardening of their hearts. They are unreasonable children that do not know what they want. Now there is one here who performs signs,—but even on his testimony they do not believe the nearness of the Kingdom. So the curse upon Chorazin and Bethsaida concludes the "eulogy upon the Baptist."

The sending of the Twelve was the last effort for bringing about the Kingdom. As they then returned, announced to him their success, and reported that they had power over the evil spirits, it signified to him, *all is ready.* So now he expects the dawn of the Kingdom in the most immediate future,—it had seemed to him, indeed, already doubtful whether the Twelve would return before this event. He had even said to them that the appearing of the Son of Man would overtake them before they had gone through the cities of Israel.

His work is done. Now he requires to collect himself and to be alone with his Disciples. They enter a boat and sail along the coast towards the north. But the multitude which had gathered about him at the preaching of the Disciples, in order to await the Kingdom with him, now follow after them along the shore and surprise them at their landing upon a lonely beach.

As it was evening the Disciples desired that he would send the people away to find food in the neighbouring hamlets. For him, however, the hour is too solemn to be profaned by an earthly meal. Before sending them away he bids them sit down and celebrates with them an anticipation of the messianic feast. To the community that was gathered about him to await the Kingdom, he, the Messiah to be, distributes hallowed food, mysteriously consecrating them thereby to be partakers of the heavenly banquet. As they did not know his secret, they understood as little as did his Disciples the significance of his act. They comprehended only that it meant something wonderfully solemn, and they questioned within themselves about it.

Thereupon he sent them away. He ordered the Disciples to skirt the coast to Bethsaida. For his part he betook himself to the mountain to pray and then followed along the shore on foot. As his figure appeared to them in the obscurity of the night they believed—under the impression of the Supper where he stood before them in mysterious majesty—that his supernatural apparition approached them over the turbulent waves through which they were toiling to the shore.

The morning after the Supper by the seashore he collected the people and the Disciples about him at Bethsaida and warned them to stand by him and not to deny him in the humiliation.

Six days later he goes with the Three to the mountain where he had prayed alone. There he is revealed to them as the Messiah. On the way home he forbade them to say anything about it until at the Resurrection he should be revealed in the glory of the Son of Man. They, however, still remark the failure of Elijah to appear, who yet must come before the Resurrection of the dead can take place. They were not present at the eulogy over the Baptist to hear the mysterious intimation he let fall. He must therefore make it clear to them now that the beheaded prisoner was Elijah. They should take no offence at his fate, for it was so ordained. He also who is to be Son of Man must suffer many things and be set at naught. So the Scripture will have it.

The Kingdom which Jesus expected so very soon failed to make its appearance. This first eschatological delay and postponement was momentous for the fate of the Gospel tradition, inasmuch as now all the events related to the mission of the Twelve became unintelligible, because all consciousness was lost of the fact that the most intense eschatological expectation then inspired Jesus and his following. Hence it is that precisely this period is confused and obscure in the accounts, and all the more so because several incidents remained enigmatical to those even who had a part in the experience. Thus the sacramental Supper by the seashore became in the tradition a "miraculous feeding," in a sense totally different from that which Jesus had in mind.

Therewith, too, the motives of Jesus' disappearance became unintelligible. It seems to be a case of flight, while on the other hand the accounts give no hint how matters had come to such a pass. The key to the historical understanding of the life of Jesus lies in the perception of the two corresponding points at which the eschatological expectation culminated. During the days at Jerusalem there was a return of the enthusiasm which had already showed itself in the days at Bethsaida. Without this assumption we are left with a yawning gap in the Gospel tradition between the mission of the Twelve and the journey to Jerusalem. Historians find themselves compelled to *invent* a period of Galilean defeat in order to establish some connection between the recorded facts,—as if a section were missing in our Gospels. *That is the weak point of all the "lives of Jesus."*

By his retreat into the region of the Genesareth Jesus withdrew himself from the Pharisees and the people in order to be alone with his Disciples, as he had in vain tried to do since their return from their mission. He urgently needed such a retreat, for he had to come to an understanding about two messianic facts.

Why is the Baptist executed by the secular authority before the messianic time has dawned?

Why does the Kingdom fail to appear notwithstanding that the tokens of its dawning are present?

The secret is made known to him through the Scripture: God brings the Kingdom about *without the general Affliction.* He whom God has destined to reign in glory accomplishes it upon himself by being tried as a malefactor and condemned. Wherefore the others go free: he makes the atonement for them. What though they believe that God punishes him, though they become offended in him who preached unto them righteousness,—when after his Passion the glory dawns, then shall they see that he has suffered for them.

Thus Jesus read in the Prophet Isaiah what God had

determined for him, the Elect. The end of the Baptist showed him in what form he was destined to suffer this condemnation: he must be put to death by the secular authority as a malefactor in the sight of all the people. Therefore he must make his way up to Jerusalem for the season when all Israel is gathered there.

As soon therefore as the time came for the Passover pilgrimage he set out with his Disciples. Before they left the north country he asked them whom the people took him to be. For reply they could only say that he was taken for Elijah. But Peter, mindful of the revelation on the mountain near Bethsaida, said: Thou art the Son of God. Whereupon Jesus informed them of his secret. Yes, he it is who shall be revealed as Son of Man at the Resurrection. But before that, it is decreed that he must be delivered to the high priests and elders to be condemned and put to death. God so wills it. For this cause they are going up to Jerusalem.

Peter resents this new disclosure, for in the revelation on the mountain there was nothing said to such an effect. He takes Jesus apart and appeals to him energetically. Whereupon he is sharply rebuked as one who gives ear to human considerations when God speaks.

This journey to Jerusalem was the funeral march to victory. Within the secret of the Passion lay concealed the secret of the Kingdom. They marched after him, and knew only that when all this was accomplished he would be Messiah. They were sorrowful for what must come to pass; they did not understand why it must be so, and they durst not ask him. But above all, their thoughts were occupied about the conditions that awaited them in the approaching Kingdom. When once he was Messiah, what would they then be? That occupied their minds, and about it they talked with one another. But he reproved them and explained why he must suffer. Only through humiliation and the meek sacrifice of service is one prepared to reign in the Kingdom of God. Therefore must he, who shall exercise supreme authority as Son of Man, make now an atonement for many by giving up his life in meek sacrifice.

With the arrival upon the Jewish territory begins the second period of Jesus' public ministry. He is again surrounded by the people. In Jericho a multitude gathers to see him pass through. By the healing of a blind beggar, the son of Timæus, the people are convinced that he is the great Forerunner, just as they thought already in Galilee. The jubilant multitudes prepare for him a festal entry into Jerusalem. As the one who according to prophecy precedes the Messiah they acclaim him with *Hosanna. Hosanna in the highest,* however, is their acclaim of the Kingdom about to appear. Therewith the same situation is reached again as in the great days near Bethsaida: Jesus is thronged by the multitudes expectant of the Kingdom.

The instruction contained in the parables which were uttered at Jerusalem has to do with the nearness of the Kingdom. They are cries of warning, with a note of menace as well for those that harden their hearts against the message. What agitates men's minds is not the question, Is he the Messiah, or no? but, Is the Kingdom so near as he says, or no?

The Pharisees and Scribes knew not what hour had struck. They showed a complete lack of sensibility for the nearness of the Kingdom, for else they could not have propounded to him questions which in view of the advanced hour had lost all significance. What difference does it make now about the Roman tribute? What do the far-fetched Sadduceean arguments amount to against the possibility of the resurrection of the dead? Soon, with the advent of the Kingdom, all earthly rule is done away, as well as the earthly human nature itself.

If only they understood the signs of the times! He proposes to them two questions, which should cause them to ponder and hence take note that the time they live in is pregnant with a great secret which is not dreamed of in the learning of the Scribes.

By what authority did the Baptist act? If they but knew that he was the Forerunner, as Jesus had mysteriously suggested to the people, then they must know too that the hour of the Kingdom had struck.

How is the Messiah at one time David's Son—that is, subordinate to him; at another, David's Lord—that is, his superior? If they could explain that, then would they understand also how he who now labours lowly and unknown in behalf of God's Kingdom shall be revealed as Lord and Christ.

But as it is they do not even suspect that the messianic indications harbour *secrets.* With all their learning they are blind leaders of the blind, who, instead of making the people receptive for the Kingdom, harden their hearts, and instead of drawing out from the Law the higher morality which renders men meet for the Kingdom, labour against it with their petty outward precepts and draw the people after them to perdition. Hence: Woe to the Pharisees and scribes!

True, even among them are such as have kept an open eye. The scribe who put to him the question about the great commandment and welcomed his reply is commended as "having understanding" and therefore "not far from the Kingdom of God,"—for he shall belong to it when it appears.

But the mass of the Pharisees and scribes understand

him so little that they decree his death. They had no effective charge to bring against his behaviour. A disrespectful word about the Temple—that was all. *Then Judas betrayed to them the secret.* Now he was condemned.

In the neighbourhood of death Jesus draws himself up to the same triumphant stature as in the days by the seaside,—for with death comes the Kingdom. On that occasion he had celebrated with the believers a mystic feast as an anticipation of the messianic banquet; so now he rises at the end of the last earthly supper and distributes to the Disciples hallowed food and drink, intimating to them with a solemn voice that this is the last earthly meal, for they are soon to be united at the banquet in the Father's Kingdom. Two corresponding parables suggest the secret of the Passion. For him, the bread and wine which he hands them at the Supper are his body and his blood, for by the sacrifice of himself unto death he ushers in the messianic feast. The parabolic saying remained obscure to the Disciples. It was also not intended for them, its purpose was not to explain anything to them,—*for it was an enigma-parable.*

Now, as the great hour approaches, he seeks again, as after the Supper by the seashore, a lonely spot where he may pray. He bears the Affliction for others. Therefore he can say to the Disciples beforehand that in the night they shall all be offended in him—and he does not need to condemn them, for the Scripture had so determined it. What endless peace lies in this word! Indeed, he comforts *them:* after the Resurrection he will gather them about him and go before them in messianic glory unto Galilee, retracing the same road along which they had followed him on his way to death.

It still remained, however, within the scope of God's omnipotence to eliminate the Affliction for him also.

Wherefore, as once he prayed with the believers, "And lead us not into the Temptation," so now he prays for himself, that God may permit the cup of suffering to pass his lips by. True, if it be God's will, he feels himself strong enough to drink it. He is sorrowful rather for the Three. The sons of Zebedee, to gain the seats upon the throne, have boasted that they can drink with him the cup of suffering and receive with him the baptism of suffering. Peter swore that he would stand by him even if he must die with him. He knows not what God has ordained for them,—whether he will lay upon them what they desire to undertake. Therefore he bids them remain near him. And while he prays God for himself he thinks of them and twice wakes them up, bidding them remain awake and beseech God that he may not lead them through the Temptation.

The third time he comes to them the betrayer with his band is near. The hour is come,—therefore he draws himself up to the full stature of his majesty. He is alone, his Disciples flee.

The hearing of witnesses is merely a pretence. After they have gone the High Priest puts directly the question about the messiahship. "I am," said Jesus, referring them at the same time to the hour when he shall appear as Son of Man on the clouds of heaven surrounded by the angels. Therefore he was found guilty of blasphemy and condemned to death.

On the afternoon of the fourteenth of Nisan, as they ate the Paschal lamb at even, he uttered a loud cry and died.

Postscript

The judgments passed upon this realistic account of the life of Jesus may be very diverse, according to the dogmatic, historical, or literary point of view of the critics. Only, with the *aim* of the book may they not find fault: *to depict the figure of Jesus in its overwhelming heroic greatness and to impress it upon the modern age and upon the modern theology.*

The heroic recedes from our modern *Weltanschauung*, our Christianity, and our conception of the person of Jesus. Wherefore men have humanised and humbled him. Renan has stripped off his halo and reduced him to a sentimental figure, coward spirits like Schopenhauer have dared to appeal to him for their enervating philosophy, and our generation has modernised him, with the notion that it could comprehend his character and development psychologically.

We must go back to the point where we can feel again the heroic in Jesus. Before the mysterious Person, who, in the form of his time, knew that he was creating upon the foundation of his life and death a moral world *which bears his name,* we must be forced to lay our faces in the dust, without daring even to wish to understand his nature. Only then can the heroic in our Christianity and in our *Weltanschauung* be again revived.